73 Sarraute: Portrait d'un inconnu *and* Vous les entendez?

Critical Guides to French Texts

EDITED BY ROGER LITTLE, DAVID WILLIAMS,
WOLFGANG VAN EMDEN

NATHALIE SARRAUTE

Portrait d'un inconnu
and

Vous les entendez?

Sheila M. Bell

Lecturer in French
University of Kent at Canterbury

Grant & Cutler Ltd
1 9 8 8

ISBN 0-7293-0292-X

I.S.B.N. 84-599-2548-X

DEPÓSITO LEGAL: V. 2.677- 1988

Printed in Spain by
Artes Gráficas Soler, S.A., Valencia

for

GRANT & CUTLER LTD
55-57, GREAT MARLBOROUGH STREET, LONDON W1V 2AY

Contents

To Alissa

Prefatory Note

REFERENCES to *Portrait d'un inconnu* and *Vous les entendez?* are to the Folio editions (Paris: Gallimard, 1977 and 1976 respectively). References to works listed in the Select Bibliography give the number of the work as it appears in the list in italics, followed by the page numbers in roman, thus: *6*, pp. 24-32.

1

Introduction

Nathalie Sarraute's public career as a writer began in 1939, when she was 39, with the publication of *Tropismes*, a volume of brief fictional texts or prose poems. Critical recognition was slow in coming at first. Finished in 1937, refused until 1939, *Tropismes* met with little attention: one review in the *Gazette de Liège* and a few encouraging letters, including one from the poet Max Jacob and one from Sartre. *Portrait d'un inconnu*, her first full-length novel, which was written during and after the war and published in 1948, equally went relatively unnoticed, despite a laudatory preface by Sartre, and the unsold copies were destroyed by the publisher, Robert Marin. It was not until the 1950s, and then as one of the group of *nouveaux romanciers*, that she began to establish a reputation. Two further novels and a volume of critical essays, *L'Ere du soupçon*, appeared in that decade; *Tropismes* and *Portrait* were republished. International acclaim came in 1964 with the award of the Prix international de littérature, a short-lived but prestigious prize (Beckett and Borges were fellow-prizewinners), for her fourth novel, *Les Fruits d'or*. Her association with the *nouveau roman* made for over-simplified and perverse readings of her work and her efforts to distance herself from the group have led over the years to a certain isolation. She has not been discouraged: in the sixties and seventies, she continued to publish novels and plays at her own deliberate pace, averaging one fictional text every four years, *Entre la vie et la mort* in 1968, *Vous les entendez?* in 1972, *'disent les imbéciles'* in 1976, *L'Usage de la parole* in 1980, and in the intervening years, a radio play, usually relating to the previous novel in subject-matter. Her reputation has grown with each successive work, though she long continued to be the victim of misreadings: 'Les critiques n'y comprennent rien même maintenant', she claimed in 1974, with some justification. More recent criticism has learnt to rate her work on its merits, unencumbered by notions more appropriate to other *nouveaux romanciers,* and has been aided therein by developments in critical theory where fiction is concerned.[1] She is now recognized as one of France's major living writers: at least one reviewer of her memoirs, *Enfance,* published in 1983, canvassed the possibility of her election to the *Académie française.*

Few authors contrive, in their first published work, to establish as firmly as does Nathalie Sarraute in *Tropismes* the parameters of their fictional world. Looking back on it in 1964, she herself says as much in her preface to the second edition of *L'Ere du soupçon:* 'Mon premier livre contenait en germe tout ce que, dans mes ouvrages suivants, je n'ai cessé de développer' (*16,* p. 9). In the essays of *L'Ere du soupçon* (written between 1947 and 1956), the terms 'mouvements' or 'drames' are used to identify the psychological material which interests her. Subsequently, however, when *Tropismes* became more widely known through its second edition of 1957, that term came to be adopted as an alternative and gradually lost the inverted commas which at first indicated its original status as quotation or metaphor. The term belongs originally to the natural sciences. The Oxford English Dictionary gives the following definition: 'the turning of an organism, or a part of one, in a particular direction (either in the way of growth, bending or locomotion), in response to some special stimulus, as that of light, heat, gravity, etc.' For Sarraute, the term was an approximation, a 'désignation globale très vague et grossière' (*23,* p. 34), though no more so perhaps than any attempt at labelling, and it was of course to be understood metaphorically. Her fiction is concerned not with physiology but with psychology. The preface to the 1964 edition of *L'Ere du soupçon* provides a gloss: 'Ce sont des

[1] Much of this recent work has been in English: see bibliography for titles by Britton, Jefferson, Minogue.

mouvements indéfinissables, qui glissent très rapidement aux limites de notre conscience; ils sont à l'origine de nos gestes, de nos paroles, des sentiments que nous manifestons, que nous croyons éprouver et qu'il est possible de définir. Ils me paraissaient et me paraissent encore constituer la source secrète de notre existence' (*16*, p. 8). Sarraute's creative endeavour is concerned with the exploration and expression of this 'source secrète'. Psychological tropisms, like the biological variety, result from external stimuli: 'ces drames intérieurs (...) ont tous ceci de commun, qu'ils ne peuvent se passer de partenaire' (*15*, p. 99). The partner, generally speaking, is another human being: any encounter between two human psyches will be the scene of tropistic activity. On the surface, the evidence may be minimal: an apparently anodyne phrase, a tone of voice, a fleeting expression may betray, or provoke, subterranean activity: for the father of *Portrait d'un inconnu,* the sounds of his daughter's approach are sufficient stimulus: 'quand il entend seulement le chatouillement de sa clé dans la serrure ou son petit coup de sonnette rapide, mordant, ou, venant de l'entrée, sa voix amenuisée, si douce, ou simplement dès qu'il sent – il a des antennes si sensibles – son approche, sa présence silencieuse derrière le mur' (p. 59). An outsider, even a protagonist, may fail to notice such signs or refuse to allow them any significance; for the experienced and willing reader of tropisms, however, visible or audible signs may not even be necessary: 'des ondes que nous seuls pouvons capter, sans que rien ne paraisse au-dehors, nous sont transmises directement...' (*7*, p. 115). For Sarraute, tropisms belong to the conscious rather than the unconscious mind; otherwise, she argues, she would not have been aware of their existence. Yet people seem reluctant to recognize them: 'J'ai eu l'idée de noter ces *Tropismes,* en remarquant autour de moi des êtres lisses comme des cailloux, des créatures sans faille apparente, pourtant remués imperceptiblement jusque dans leurs régions les plus profondes par des sentiments auxquels ils refusent de donner droit de cité' (*18*, p. 60). Such resistance may be offered in self-defence. At the level of tropisms, the mind is engaged in emotive or instinctive, rather than reflective, activity. It enters into such close contact with another psyche that it feels itself vulnerable, in constant danger of violation. This psychic vulnerability translates itself into innumerable tiny movements of approach and withdrawal, *bonds* and *reculs*. The world of tropisms reveals itself as a world of intense and constantly renewed drama: 'ces drames intérieurs faits d'attaques, de triomphes, de reculs, de défaites, de caresses, de morsures, de viols, de meurtres, d'abandons généreux ou d'humbles soumissions' (*15,* p. 99). It is not surprising that people cling to the surface world of clear-cut definitions and recognizable emotions, where they retain a measure of control. For Sarraute, however, it is these intersubjective reactions 'dont le jeu incessant constitue la trame invisible de tous les rapports humains' (*15,* p. 29).

Sarraute has always maintained that it is the awareness of a psychic phenomenon, as yet undefined, which is the point of departure of her work, that its original source is a non-verbal sensation. In 1971, a colloquium was held at Cerisy under the title *Nouveau roman: hier, aujourd'hui,* in which Sarraute took part. Her work was allotted a place of honour on the opening day, but her uneasy sense of not belonging was betrayed by her reluctance to attend and her departure at the end of that first day. Her own contribution is largely concerned with defining – and defending – her views in relation to the very different ones held by those in whose company she found herself. She believes, she says, in the existence of a world before language, believes that we can be dimly aware of mental sensations before these are formulated in words. In the subsequent discussion, she declares that such a belief is vital to her survival as a writer: 'Même si c'est une erreur – ce que je ne crois pas – elle m'est nécessaire. J'en ai un besoin vital. Je ne peux pas y renoncer. Dire: il n'y a pas de pré-langage, tout part des mots ... cela m'est absolument impossible'.[2] To render the 'trame invisible' visible to others, however, the intervention of language is necessary. Sarraute is equally unhappy with any account of her work which plays down the inventive role of the writer: 'Je ne crois pas que

[2] I quote from a corrected version supplied to me by Sarraute.

pour moi le roman soit jamais l'imitation d'une réalité, même inconnue. Comme Robbe-Grillet, je m'efforce de faire surgir ce qui n'existait pas avant d'être mis en forme. (...) Il me semble que les tropismes sont précisément ce "rien" qui, hors de la forme, du langage ne paraît pas avoir d'existence. Ainsi j'appelle une de mes pièces "ou ce qui s'appelle rien" ' (from a letter to the present writer). Exploration of the human psyche, work with language, these coexist in a paradoxical, mutually stimulating relationship and have equally important roles to play in her work.

Like other writers before her, Sarraute is involved in a constant struggle to preserve the originality of her vision against the deadening influence of conventional discourse. She is forced to use words to communicate her insights to others, but words, by their very nature, are already endowed with meanings: 'A peine cette chose informe, toute tremblante et flageolante, cherche-t-elle à se montrer au jour qu'aussitôt ce langage si puissant et si bien armé, qui se tient toujours prêt à intervenir pour rétablir l'ordre – son ordre – saute sur elle et l'écrase' (*23,* p. 37). One of her modes of defence is to attack. Her novels scrutinize conventional discourse relating to the areas which interest her and, by juxtaposing her own alternative discourse, show the former to be inadequate, concealing more than it reveals. Under such scrutiny, such 'maniacal attentiveness' (*19,* p. 371), even platitudes take on fresh resonances; 'les mots de la tribu' become once again suitable vehicles for poetry. The letter from Max Jacob, which Sarraute received on the first publication of *Tropismes,* saluted her as a fellow-poet. If we may define the poetic writer as one who extends the expressive power of language, Nathalie Sarraute's subsequent work has amply justified Jacob's description of her.

The two novels I have chosen to examine in detail, *Portrait d'un inconnu* and *Vous les entendez?,* both explore the world of tropisms. The latter is described in the *prière d'insérer* (composed by the author) as 'une nouvelle étape sur le long et lent parcours que Nathalie Sarraute a entrepris de suivre depuis son premier ouvrage, *Tropismes*'. Thus they exemplify Sarraute's fidelity to the same general subject area throughout her creative endeavour. There are moreover particular points of similarity between these two novels: in both, a relationship between father and offspring is explored and an effort is made to preserve the truth of that relationship against the petrifying effect of words. *Vous les entendez?* is however 'une nouvelle étape' and the striking differences which exist between it and *Portrait* will allow us to emphasize Nathalie Sarraute's development as a novelist and the increasing confidence and skill with which she depicts her chosen area. By comparison with *Vous les entendez?*, *Portrait* is a hesitant, self-justificatory work. It is concerned to situate its human figures in relation to the mainstay of the traditional novel: the character. Its title points up the difference: in contrast to the great realist novels of the nineteenth century which offer us confidently César Birotteau, Adam Bede or Anna Karenina, we have here the portrait of an unknown man. The portrait has a painter: standing between Nathalie Sarraute and the reader of *Portrait* is a surrogate author figure, a first-person narrator, who acts as guide and interpreter. His role is that of 'corps conducteur à travers lequel passaient tous les courants dont l'atmosphère était chargée' (p. 131); he conjures up for us what he senses of the tropistic mental activity of others: 'Je sentais que certains mots qu'on prononçait ouvraient de vastes entonnoirs, d'immenses précipices, visibles aux seuls initiés qui se penchaient, se retenaient – et je me penchais avec eux, me retenais, tremblant comme eux et attiré – au-dessus du vide' (p. 132). We follow the narrator's gaze and share in his vision. We may eventually feel, however, that the objects of his attention, the old man and his daughter, are his, not ours, theoretical figures in relation to whom we are invited to explore the narrator's aims and interests. *Vous les entendez?*, in dispensing with the narrator figure, calls for more direct participation. Here again the title is revealing. With an ambivalence which, as we shall see, is altogether characteristic of the novel as a whole, the question in the title belongs to more than one owner and signifies on more than one level. A father is asked by his friend whether he hears his children laughing: 'Vous les entendez?' The question, as received by the father, refers also to the unarticulated messages contained in the laughter. The novel, in making the phrase its title, asks the same question of its readers; do *we* hear these messages in the laughter, and, by extension, similar mental activity in the father as well? The novel seeks to articulate the messages for us, not by the intermediary of a narrator, but by translating them into modes of speech. Such a technique was already at the disposal of the narrator of *Portrait* but was only one of a number: in *Vous les entendez?*, it has invaded the whole novel, including, significantly, its title.

2

Portrait d'un inconnu

(1) THE OPENING SECTION

T H E opening section of *Portrait* offers certain guide-lines
as to how to read the novel which follows. First of all, it
prevents us from reading it as a traditional realist novel: there
are no named characters, no suggestions of plot development,
no indications of a social background to which characters and
plot may relate. A first-person narrator sets a distinctive tone,
establishes what Valerie Minogue calls 'a manner of speaking'
(cf. her account of the first paragraphs of *Portrait*: *43,* p. 33),
and it is this tone which makes the strongest impression on
the reader initially: a tone marked by an uneasy mixture of
persistence and hesitation, approach and withdrawal, conviction and self-doubt, and which induces in the reader himself a
sense of unease. This narrator does not introduce himself to
us, not even in the ironic mode which frequently characterizes the first-person narrator in twentieth-century fiction. [3]
We are not told and will never know exactly who is the I who
speaks to us: culturally he would seem to belong to the
educated classes, but he has no profession, no precise age, the
most minimal of family circles – 'mes vieux parents' (p. 72) –
and as supreme indication of his 'otherness', no proper
name (see *38,* for a discussion of the importance of this
feature).

[3] Cf. Salinger's Holden Caulfield in *The Catcher in the Rye*: 'The first
thing you'll probably want to know is where I was born, and what my lousy
childhood was like (...), and all that David Copperfield kind of crap, but I
don't feel like going into it'.

The first few pages of the novel make it clear to us that there are three important elements in this strange fictional world: the narrator, his material and his audience or rather audiences (in the second half of the section, he addresses himself to another group from which he expects and gets much more cooperation). The narrator seeks, whether as professional story-teller or simply as amateur psychologist, to give an account of something or someone to a third party. He feels 'the excitement which a writer feels in front of certain things [and] which makes him want to show these things to others' (*21*, p. 428); he is fascinated by his subject-matter and cannot resist trying to communicate his fascination, even though he knows he will be unsuccessful: the situation is a familiar one to him, he has found himself in it many times before, knows, as he gives in to the impulse, what the outcome will be. His own feelings regarding the subject-matter are ambivalent: he is fascinated but also repelled; he feels sympathy for the reluctance of his first audience to be drawn and distaste for his second, who appear too readily converted to his point of view: there is in him 'quelque chose de louche', whereas their world is 'normal, décent'. His material, it gradually emerges in the course of this section, consists of two human beings, referred to by him as 'elle' and 'lui' (or 'le vieux'). The comments of others suggest that these are a father and his daughter. But he himself is not concerned with what such labels can express about them but with what he senses of their inner mental life when he comes into contact with them. Such are the perceptions he tries to offer his audience, as the novel opens: 'Je leur ai demandé s'ils ne sentaient pas comme moi, s'ils n'avaient pas senti, parfois, quelque chose de bizarre, une vague émanation, quelque chose qui sortait d'elle et se collait à eux' (p. 17). Even when he receives as response the evasive and discouraging, 'Je la trouve un peu ennuyeuse', he persists: 'n'avaient-ils pas senti, parfois, quelque chose qui sortait d'elle, quelque chose de mou, de gluant, qui adhérait et aspirait sans qu'on sache comment et qu'il fallait soulever et arracher de sa peau comme une compresse humide à l'odeur fade, douceâtre' (p. 18). What he seeks, it would appear, is to provoke rejection rather than agreement, 'un de ces mots-réflexes (...) comme un coup de poing de boxeur', and he provides some examples: 'C'est un vieil égoïste, disent-elles, je l'ai toujours dit, un égoïste et un grippe-sou, des gens comme ça ne devraient pas avoir le droit de mettre au monde des enfants. Et elle, c'est une maniaque. Elle n'est pas responsable. Moi je dis qu'elle est plutôt à plaindre, la pauvre fille' (p. 19).

The narrator's own perceptions are conveyed in part by metaphor: 'toutes ces comparaisons avec les compresses humides et les odeurs douceâtres, avec tout ce qui s'accroche, adhère à vous, s'infiltre, vous tire à votre insu' (pp. 20-21). Such images are not to be taken too seriously: they are a way of communicating with the uninitiated. The narrator's perceptions are also conveyed by negative means, by comparison with other ways of seeing which are radically different from his. The outlook represented by his first audience is made more tangible by being identified with certain types of people, women neighbours, for example, who stop for a brief gossip: 'deux femmes qui se croisent sur le seuil de la porte ou bien dans l'escalier, leur filet à la main, pressées de sortir, de rentrer, préoccupées' (p. 19). This audience deals in precise labels which sum people up and express judgments upon them. The narrator has an alternative audience to whom he can turn if he wants an entirely different reaction. As against the men in the street (or women) of the first pages, the members of this audience are much more sophisticated and are ready to listen and to sympathize (to the narrator's dismay, for he always hopes they will side with the others against him). Here we have intellectuals, aesthetes, not perhaps for the time being interested in 'les endroits obscurs de la psychologie' (*15*, p. 81), but nonetheless able and willing, apparently, to meet him on his own ground. But the narrator rapidly finds that this audience distorts his vision, reduces it to the familiar, the *déjà vu*. They too impose a grill on 'elle' and 'le vieux'; they make of them psychological monsters, monsters who develop and flourish in the enclosed, stifling world of the provincial, middle-class family, and who have become familiar to us from the novels of Julien Green and Mauriac as well as from the occasional court case or public scandal. The narrator's second audience makes this familiarity explicit. They recall a visit to the apartment of father and daughter, 'un vieil appartement avec des meubles 1900, des rideaux jaunes, brise-bise, très petit-bourgeois, donnant sur une cour sombre probablement (...) L'ensemble faisait assez dans le genre de Julien Green ou de Mauriac' (p. 23). They equally read the relationship in terms of a true story, that of the *séquestrée de Poitiers,* perhaps the most famous of such family scandals: 'Ils rient ... "Ils devaient jouir de cela, elle et le vieux, tous les deux enfermés là sans vouloir en sortir, reniflant leurs propres odeurs, bien chaudement calfeutrés dans leur grand fond de Malempia" ' (p. 23).[4] The narrator's vision is thus identified with a fascination for abnormal psychology, catered for by a particular fictional tradition, or more successfully still, by the *fait divers.* The second audience, like the first, is reductive, even if one is sought out by the narrator and the other rejected in disgust.

Our opening section then presents us with two kinds of psychological movement on the part of the narrator himself. In the first, he seeks contact with his audience, only to be kept at arm's length, reduced to listening at doors or hanging about on the floor above, hoping to overhear the sort of confident judgment for which he longs; finally rejected, he has to withdraw with as much dignity as he can muster. In the second, he again advances, only then to react against the

---

[4] The phrase 'leur grand fond de Malempia' provides a short-hand reference to the story of this woman who was imprisoned for 25 years by her mother and brother in an indescribably squalid, vermin-infested room. She was discovered and released in 1901. The phrase is a transcription of the incomprehensible sounds used by the woman to refer to her room and her former life within it; by extension it came to identify – without attempting to explain – the mysterious bond linking the members of the family together. Gide's essay on the case, *La Séquestrée de Poitiers,* published in 1930, provoked renewed interest in it. Sarraute herself refers to it elsewhere (*15,* p. 66). Gide's aim was of course itself subversive, to offer his reader examples of actions 'dont les motifs restent mystérieux, échappent aux règles de la psychologie traditionnelle' (Folio, p. 99). Here, however, the story has itself become conventional, a crude over-simplification, an example of what the second audience offers, 'de vieilles réminiscences de faits divers, de grosses "tranches de vie" aux couleurs lourdes, trop simples' (p. 24).

contact which is made, to feel threatened, polluted, violated:
'ils prennent n'importe quoi et ils l'étalent sur moi, ils
m'empoignent n'importe comment' (p. 24). Thus we have in
the opening section not only the central elements of the
fiction, a narrator, his material and the notion of an audience,
a receiver of the tale, but also a paradigm of the psychological
movements the narrator will seek to follow in the rest of the
book, tropistic movements of attraction and repulsion.

(2) FIGURES OF AUTHORITY

The opening section presents us with a narrator who
seems instinctively to feel that authority lies elsewhere, who
sees himself as an outcast, unworthy, fit only to gather up the
crumbs from under the table of the elect. He is in the
ambivalent position of challenging values set by authority,
yet hoping that his challenge will be defeated, denied, ruled
out of court. His feelings are compared to those he suffered as
a child, when some decree of his parents was challenged:
'j'aurais préféré mille fois que, contre toute justice, contre
toute évidence, on me donne tort à moi, pour que tout reste
normal, décent, pour que je puisse avoir, comme les autres,
de vrais parents à qui on peut se soumettre, en qui on peut
avoir confiance' (pp. 21-22). There are two representatives of
authority in the novel who appear in the third and fourth
sections: Tolstoy, as giant among novelists and supreme
creator of *personnages,* and the 'spécialiste', as expert in the
arrière-fond of the human psyche. Each may be seen as
standing behind one of the audiences of the opening section,
supplying their justification.

Before we encounter these figures, in the second section of
the novel, we see the narrator in action; here again, we find
patterns which are characteristic of the novel as a whole: he
meets the daughter, seeks to fathom her reactions and to
follow her in mind as she leaves him to go to her father, and
finally tries, with little sense of success, to express his discov-
eries in words for the benefit of a friend (or for his own
benefit, since it is equally possible to read in that way the

figure of the 'alter'). A second encounter takes place as the
daughter suddenly reappears, now herself, it would seem, in
the role of aggressor; a similar attempt at psychological
pursuit ensues. Then, in the third section, the narrator shifts
to the father's point of view and imagines the reception of the
daughter from his angle. He has the sense that the father
wears a mask in the presence of his daughter, perhaps has
always done so since first seeing her in her cradle, and he
speculates on the reasons for this. These are difficult to
fathom and are dismissed by most people as unworthy of
interest: 'Je n'en sais rien. Personne n'en sait rien. Personne
ne s'en est jamais préoccupé. Ils ont tous d'autres chats à
fouetter, d'autres préoccupations plus louables, plus légiti-
mes. Même ceux qui semblent avoir touché à cette question
n'ont jamais daigné s'y arrêter' (p. 62). One of these last is
Tolstoy and the narrator proceeds to examine two of the
characters of *War and Peace,* Prince Bolkonski and his
daughter Marie, in the light of his theory of masks. What lies
beneath the prince's brusque, even surly manner with his
daughter, the gentle, long-suffering Marie? How does this
manner relate to his words of tenderness to her at the
moment of his death? Was it perhaps something in Marie
which normally inhibited her father, making him brusque
rather than tender? Such questions remain unanswered despite the narrator's efforts. Tolstoy's characters are resistant
to his attempts to penetrate below their surface:

> De bien plus forts que moi se casseraient les ongles, les
> dents, à essayer ainsi, insolemment, de s'attaquer au prince
> Bolkonski ou à la princesse Marie.
> Ils sont, ne l'oublions pas, des personnages. De ces person-
> nages de roman si réussis que nous disons d'eux habituelle-
> ment qu'ils sont 'réels', 'vivants', plus 'réels' même et plus
> 'vivants' que les gens vivants eux-mêmes.   (pp. 64-65)

Of such characters, we retain clear, precise images, which
appear to guarantee their reality: 'la botte, par exemple, la
botte souple en cuir tartare, ornée de broderies d'argent, qui
chaussait le pied du vieux prince, ou sa courte pelisse de

velours bordée d'un col de zibeline et son bonnet, ou ses mains osseuses et dures qui serraient comme des pinces, ses petites mains sèches de vieillard, aux veines saillantes' (p. 65). Not only are such characters too strong for the narrator but he has a nostalgic longing that his own creatures might assume such firmness and clarity; the terms of the comparison he makes reflect his feelings: 'Comme je voudrais leur voir aussi ces formes lisses et arrondies, ces contours purs et fermes, à ces lambeaux informes, ces ombres tremblantes, ces spectres, ces goules, ces larves qui me narguent et après lesquels je cours...' (p. 66). But this is not possible: even the first tentative step of giving them a proper name is beyond him.

Behind the women with their shopping (pp. 19, 57) and their pronouncements on the old man and his daughter, stands then the impressive figure of the Tolstoyan fictional character, guaranteeing the propriety of such labels and judgments. Sarraute chose Tolstoy because his fiction, and *War and Peace* in particular, possesses an exemplary status for many people. She writes in an article of 1960 on Tolstoy:

> Je l'ai si bien senti qu'en 1943 quand j'écrivais *Portrait d'un inconnu,* j'ai choisi comme modèles parfaits de personnages de roman, de personnages 'vivants' admirablement réussis, deux personnages de *Guerre et Paix,* le vieux prince Bolkonski et sa fille. Je les ai choisis pour les opposer dans leur perfection à ce qu'étaient devenus les personnages, après toutes les dislocations et désintégrations qu'ils n'avaient cessé de subir à travers le roman contemporain. Je voulais montrer que chercher à imiter ces modèles, c'était aller à contre-courant de l'évolution de la littérature de notre temps.   (*20,* p. 1)

The shadow of Balzac also looms beside that of Tolstoy; when avarice is linked with fatherhood, no explicit reference is necessary: the comparisons with Balzac are inevitable. *Eugénie Grandet* was certainly in Nathalie Sarraute's mind as she wrote *Portrait d'un inconnu*:

The situation was like the one chosen by Balzac in *Eugénie Grandet*. Of course I did not try to compete with Balzac's masterpiece. But I thought that what we know about reality has changed since Balzac's time. In *Portrait of a Man Unknown* characters appeared from the outside as they appear in the traditional novel: the father was a miser, an egoist, the daughter a cranky spinster. This was what people said about them. But what did it really mean? What kind of movements composed what appeared on the surface as something that could be labelled: an egoist, a miser? What kind of tropisms take place in a man whom others, when they speak about him, call a miser? This was what the narrator, who spoke in the first person, wanted to know.   (*21*, p. 429)

This is not to suggest that a theoretical argument relating to the *personnage de roman* was Sarraute's point of departure in writing fiction; that was rather personal experience stretching back into childhood. Nonetheless, as she worked, one of her *points de repère* became the classic fictional character. As a result of writing *Portrait* and finding it ignored or misunderstood, she pursued a concern with this theme into her critical essays. It is the subject in particular of 'L'Ere du soupçon', which was first published in February 1950. Her point of departure in that essay is that, whatever the critics may say, novelist and reader alike have lost their faith in the *personnage de roman*:

> Depuis les temps heureux d'*Eugénie Grandet* où, parvenu au faîte de sa puissance, il trônait entre le lecteur et le romancier, objet de leur ferveur commune, tels les Saints des tableaux primitifs entre les donateurs, il n'a cessé de perdre successivement tous ses attributs et prérogatives.
> Il était très richement pourvu, comblé de biens de toute sorte, entouré de soins minutieux; rien ne lui manquait, depuis les boucles d'argent de sa culotte jusqu'à la loupe veinée au bout de son nez. Il a, peu à peu, tout perdu: ses ancêtres, sa maison soigneusement bâtie, bourrée de la cave au grenier d'objets de toute espèce, jusqu'aux plus menus colifichets, ses propriétés et ses titres de rente, ses vêtements, son corps, son visage, et, surtout, ce bien précieux entre tous,

> son caractère qui n'appartenait qu'à lui, et souvent jusqu'à
> son nom. (*15*, p. 57)

The narrator is still very much aware of the *personnage* as threat to his own vision. That he should be forced to compare his creations with that of *two* such formidable forerunners makes his own position all the more vulnerable.

The other figure of authority, proposed to us by the novel, is to be found in the next section, the 'spécialiste' (on one level clearly a psychiatrist) to whom the narrator has recourse when he feels his preoccupations are threatening to overwhelm him: 'Je suis rentré dans le rang. Il le fallait. On ne peut impunément vivre parmi les larves. Le jeu devenait malsain' (p. 68). He is a specialist in the field of psychological undercurrents and it is as such – and with ironic emphasis – that he is identified in the novel. Suggestions that the narrator may be seen as *névrosé* are present from early on. In the opening section, he gives his feelings the proper psychiatric label and there is more evidence of the same expertise later (e.g., p. 116); he is familiar, it would seem, with the devices used by doctors to manipulate their patients' mental states; he can recognize morbid symptoms and knows the way in which psychiatric cases are labelled: 'le patient est affublé pour la commodité d'un prénom familier, parfois un peu grotesque, Octave ou Jules. Ou simplement Oct. h. 35 ans' (p. 27). This readiness on the part of psychiatrists to invent proper names for their patients is in itself indicative of the gulf that exists between their way of perceiving human beings and that of the narrator. Like the second audience in the opening section, the 'spécialiste' appears to understand the narrator's preoccupations and to be ready to treat him with tact and sympathy. But it is the 'fausse solidarité doucereuse' (p. 27), to which the novel has already alluded. His attitude is reductive; he reduces the narrator's perceptions to the known, the familiar: 'C'est un trait répandu chez les névropathes, cette soumission au cliché que vous avez très bien dégagée, du reste, et qui n'a rien, à mon avis, d'inquiétant ni de mystérieux' (p. 70). When the narrator tries to discuss the example of Bolkonski with him, he is patronizing; without professing any expertise as a literary critic, he gives him good advice: 'Montrez-nous donc quelqu'un de bien vivant et collez-lui, si cela vous plaît, tous les masques que vous voudrez. Mais faites-le vivre d'abord, rendez-le concret, tangible' (p. 71). His discussion of the old man and his daughter transforms them for the narrator, and the terms in which the latter now describes them are significantly reminiscent of those used in the previous section to evoke the *personnage de roman*: '"ils" changent d'aspect, se rapprochent, deviennent durs, eux aussi, finis, avec des couleurs nettes, des contours précis, mais un peu à la manière de ces poupées en carton peint qui servent de cibles dans les foires' (p. 71), a lifelessness also, as we shall see later, identified with the *personnage de roman*. The scene which follows, in which the narrator returns to normality, reinforces the view that the specialist's treatment is destructive of life. The narrator's elderly parents seek to recreate for him the cosy, secure world of his childhood; 'en me faisant manger des éclairs au chocolat', they embark on a conversation about old friends, full of proper names and factual detail about families, houses and children. The narrator co-operates: 'je faisais pivoter devant eux, comme ils le voulaient, leurs poupées, j'avançais avec eux lentement à travers leur musée, je passais avec eux la revue de leurs soldats de plomb...' (p. 73). Ultimately, the professional is no less destructive than the gossip of the narrator's private vision.

In both these sections, the narrator's preoccupations are shown in a negative light, due in part to the attitude expressed or represented by the figure of authority, in part to the pejorative connotations of much of the terminology used to identify them: 'ces spectres, ces goules, ces larves' (p. 66), or 'ces pulsations, ces frémissements, ces tentacules qui se tendent' (p. 69). However, despite the fact that, in both encounters, it might seem as if the narrator has come off worst – thwarted in his attempts to discover the subterranean mental life of Tolstoy's characters, dismissed by the specialist as a familiar 'case', offering little in the way of interest – the final impression we take away from each is ambivalent. Just as the hostile critic of *Les Faux-monnayeurs* may find

himself disarmed by seeing his own objections formulated in
the discussion at Saas-fée, so here too the author's defences
are strengthened by allowing her narrator/novelist figure to
be explicitly attacked. We have seen how the psychiatrist
comes across as a negative presence: the tone of his utterances
reveals his sympathy to be patronizing. With Tolstoy, such
possibilities are not available, but the discussion of his characters shows signs, on the narrator's part, of a reservation
which runs counter to the nostalgic admiration he also
expresses: the inverted commas round 'réels' and 'vivants',
drawing attention to the paradoxical nature of the claim that
these creatures are more real than the people we know, the
slightly dismissive phrase, 'petites images précises et colo-
rées', to describe the means by which these figures achieve this
quality of 'reality', and the ambivalent status to which they
thereby attain: 'Ces personnages occupent dans ce vaste
musée où nous conservons les gens que nous avons connus,
aimés, et auquel nous faisons allusion, sans doute, quand
nous parlons de notre "expérience de la vie", une place de
choix' (p. 65).

Furthermore, both sections end on a note which suggests
ultimate rejection of the outlook with which the two figures
of authority have been identified. The Tolstoy section ends
with one of the most powerful passages in the novel: it retains
the terminology already used to distinguish between Tolstoy's
characters and the strange creations of the narrator's mind
and yet it can be seen as reversing the scale of values these
terms imply and finally affirming the latter's vision as that
which signifies life. The rhetoric of the passage requires that
it be cited in full:

> Ils ne sont pas pour moi, les ornements somptueux, les
> chaudes couleurs, les certitudes apaisantes, la fraîche douceur
> de la 'vie'. Pas pour moi. Moi je ne sais, quand ils daignent
> parfois s'approcher de moi aussi, ces gens 'vivants', ces per-
> sonnages, que tourner autour d'eux, cherchant avec un achar-
> nement maniaque la fente, la petite fissure, ce point fragile
> comme la fontanelle des petits enfants, où il me semble
> que quelque chose, comme une pulsation à peine perceptible,
> affleure et bat doucement. Là je m'accroche, j'appuie. Et je

> sens alors sourdre d'eux et s'écouler en un jet sans fin une
> matière étrange, anonyme comme la lymphe, comme le sang,
> une matière fade et fluide qui coule entre mes mains, qui se
> répand... Et il ne reste plus, de leur chair si ferme, colorée,
> veloutée, de gens vivants, qu'une enveloppe exsangue, informe
> et grise. (pp. 66-67)

The 'gens "vivants"', the 'personnages' are reduced to 'une
enveloppe exsangue, informe et grise', but the narrator's
'matière anonyme' shows a flicker of life and we are left with
'quelque chose, comme une pulsation à peine perceptible'. At
the end of the section concerning the visit to the specialist,
there is a similar suggestion that the narrator may rebel
against the psychiatrist's reductive, life-destroying verdict.
Again the tone is ambivalent. The narrator is weakened,
submissive; he clings to the atmosphere created by his parents' chat, for he is afraid:

> je me retenais à eux, car je commençais déjà à sentir en moi
> quelque chose qui se soulevait, quelque chose qui battait
> doucement dans le vide, se soulevait, retombait, comme cogne
> dans le silence de la nuit un volet mal fermé – je me retenais à
> eux, car je savais que si je restais seul tout à coup, sans eux,
> dans la rue chaude et vide, le battement résonnerait en moi
> atrocement fort. (pp. 73-74)

The image of the 'volet mal fermé' threatens the cosy,
'normal' world of chocolate éclairs and memories of old
friends, which his parents have been trying to construct
about him. But opposed to the 'musée' of the parents, their
dolls and lead-soldiers, is 'quelque chose qui se soulevait,
quelque chose qui battait doucement dans le vide'. The terms
of the opposition are similar to those in the previous section
and again it is suggested that, however unattractive, however
alarming its manifestations may be, life is with the narrator.

(3) THE PAINTING OF THE TITLE

We have already seen how imagery connected with life
and death is used to subvert the system of values which is

represented by the figures of authority in the novel and to which the narrator himself still intermittently appears to subscribe. Death is associated with the *personnage de roman* and with people who have passed through the hands of the psychiatrist, life with the narrator's fumbling and hesitant perceptions. Life is also, most triumphantly, associated with the painting which plays a central role in the novel, both in terms of the action and on a symbolic level. Its significance is of course underlined by the fact that it gives the novel its title. This is the painting which the narrator sees in an art-gallery, when he goes to Holland on a journey approved by the psychiatrist and his family, as a further stage in his cure.

Travel, the novel suggests, may be a way of shielding oneself against direct contact with reality. Later on, the tourist's habit of reducing each town to the object associated with it – gloves in London, tea-services in Dresden, cashmere shawls in Moscow, carpets in Constantinople (pp. 143-144) – is presented as a means of self-protection, a means of disguising 'un univers informe, étrange et menaçant' (p. 143). We have already seen the narrator employing a similar distancing device, where the streets and squares of his own neighbourhood are concerned. The secret is to place already existing images between oneself and the reality before one: 'comme on fait souvent dans les villes inconnues, appliquer sur les choses et maintenir en avant des images puisées dans des réminiscences, littéraires ou autres, des souvenirs de tableaux ou même de cartes postales dans le genre de celles où l'on peut voir écrit au verso: Paris. Bords de la Seine. Un square'. Thus the streets around him take on the air 'plein de charme, triste et tendre, des petites rues d'Utrillo' and the square in which he encounters the little old woman, could be 'un square de Haarlem ou de Bruges' (p. 29). He sets out on his journey to the Dutch town in very much the same spirit. It is not for him a real town at all (it is noticeable that no name is mentioned), but the town of Baudelaire's 'L'Invitation au voyage': 'C'était de la matière épurée, décantée' (p. 78). He wanders round the art gallery, looking at his favourite great paintings: 'Ici aussi [as with the Tolstoyan character], il n'y avait qu'à s'abandonner, qu'à prendre. L'effort, le doute, le tourment avaient été surmontés, dépassés, le but était atteint, et elles m'offraient maintenant la sérénité féconde et grave de leur sourire apaisé, la grâce exquise de leur détachement' (p. 79). Yet his visit to the art gallery, indeed his choice of this particular town, may have an ulterior motivation, a motivation which is in fact working against his cure. One particular painting has drawn him back here, a portrait of an unknown man by an unknown artist, which is very different from the masterpieces which are hung in the main rooms of the gallery:

> Il me parut, cette fois, plutôt plus étrange encore qu'il ne m'avait paru autrefois. Les lignes de son visage, de son jabot de dentelles, de son pourpoint, de ses mains, semblaient être les contours fragmentaires et incertains que découvrent à tâtons, que palpent les doigts hésitants d'un aveugle. On aurait dit qu'ici l'effort, le doute, le tourment avaient été surpris par une catastrophe soudaine et qu'ils étaient demeurés là, fixés en plein mouvement, comme ces cadavres qui restent pétrifiés dans l'attitude où la mort les a frappés. Ses yeux seuls semblaient avoir échappé au cataclysme et avoir atteint le but, l'achèvement: ils paraissaient avoir tiré à eux et concentré en eux toute l'intensité, la vie qui manquaient à ses traits encore informes et disloqués.   (p. 80)

The contrast with the *personnage de roman* (as studied in the example of Prince Bolkonski) is striking. The outer details are incomplete, unfinished, lacking all the clarity of outline, the vivid quality of the fictional character; the supposedly real, living quality, which the repeated inverted commas suggest to be conventional, is replaced by a concentrated intensity of life which speaks through the eyes and seems to have little or nothing to do with the outer shell in which it is encased. The painting and its painter speak to the narrator in a way that Tolstoy or the psychiatrist do not, in a way which, instead of rejecting the narrator's vision of things, enters into communion with it and encourages him to respond positively and joyously:

pre-language

> Et petit à petit, <u>je sentais comme en moi une note timide, un son d'autrefois, presque oublié, s'élevait,</u> hésitant d'abord. Et il me semblait, tandis que je restais là devant lui, perdu, fondu en lui, que cette note hésitante et grêle, cette réponse timide qu'il avait fait sourdre de moi, pénétrait en lui, <u>résonnait en lui,</u> il la recueillait, il la renvoyait, fortifiée, grossie par lui comme par un amplificateur, elle montait de moi, de lui, s'élevait de plus en plus fort, un chant gonflé d'espoir qui me soulevait, m'emportait...   (p. 81)

The effect on the narrator is one of <u>liberation</u>: at the end of the previous section, the encounter with the psychiatrist had sent him back to the cosy teashop world of gossip over chocolate éclairs, now the portrait sends him out to the open sea: 'J'étais libre. Les amarres étaient coupées. Je voguais, poussé vers le large' (p. 82). Moreover, he sets off without hesitation, reluctance or fear: the self-doubt which is such a constant feature of his outlook vanishes. The effect of this encounter is further explored at the beginning of the following section where the narrator's state of exultation is evoked. The imagery no longer has its familiar connotations of malaise, even disgust: the odour of the 'nourritures à moi' is 'pareil à celui qu'exhalent dans l'air printanier les jeunes feuilles mouillées de pluie' (p. 83).

Both state of mind and imagery of liberation are reminiscent of Gide, already held up as a model in the parting words of the psychiatrist to the narrator, as the latter set out on his journey: 'Soyez Nathanaël, goûtez aux "nourritures terrestres". Retrouvez – c'est ce qui vous manque maintenant pour achever la guérison – retrouvez la "ferveur"' (p. 77). Are we to assume then that the psychiatrist is now exerting a more subtle form of dominion over his patient and that the narrator has not freed himself at all? The narrator is certainly not wholly without literary allies. There are other writers, too, who are mentioned elsewhere in *Portrait,* and with whose work the narrator seems to have a special affinity: Dostoevsky, Pirandello, Rilke. Gide apart, the writer who most clearly speaks through these opening paragraphs of the sixth section is undoubtedly Marcel Proust: the 'pavés irréguliers', for example, must recall Marcel's crucial experience in the courtyard of the Hôtel de Guermantes, the 'pans de murs', Bergotte's encounter with Vermeer's *View of Delft*. The narrator's treasures in general, his 'parcelles étincelantes de vie que j'étais parvenu à capter' (p. 84), have a Proustian quality, evanescent yet permanent: 'Il y en a de toutes sortes: certains que je connais bien et d'autres qui m'avaient juste fait signe une fois, qui avaient vacillé pour moi d'un chaud et doux éclat, pendant un court instant, quand j'étais passé devant eux, au milieu d'un groupe de gens, sans pouvoir m'arrêter' (p. 84). Such a description is very reminiscent of the experiences of the child Marcel on the Guermantes walk, experiences which point towards his future discovery of his vocation as a writer: 'tout d'un coup un toit, un reflet de soleil sur une pierre, l'odeur d'un chemin me faisaient arrêter par un plaisir particulier qu'ils me donnaient, et aussi parce qu'ils avaient l'air de cacher, au-delà de ce que je voyais, quelque chose qu'ils invitaient à venir prendre et que malgré mes efforts je n'arrivais pas à découvrir' (*Du côté de chez Swann,* Folio, 1972, p. 214).

Some commentators on Sarraute's work, who have found the language of these pages difficult to reconcile with the terminology used to identify authentic (i.e. the narrator's) perception elsewhere in the novel, have argued that the liberation is not genuine. Micheline Tison Braun, for example, states firmly: 'La littérature d'évasion, d'harmonie, n'est pas une littérature authentique' (*48,* p. 79). Françoise Calin argues that, though the portrait acts as a liberating force, freeing the narrator from the constraints represented by the psychiatrist, he embarks initially on a false course: 'il s'engage sur une fausse route (...) Le Narrateur croyant avoir retrouvé son inspiration, ses Muses, ne produit qu'un pastiche. Dans cette ville baudelairienne, il se meut dans un univers de pans de mur proustiens, rêve d'oasis gidiennes' (*36,* p. 195). Even Bernard Pingaud, whose article of 1963 is one of the most outstandingly perceptive early studies of Sarraute's work, takes a similar line: 'Mais ce monde vrai, rayonnant, ouvert, n'est pas le monde réel. C'est déjà un monde *raconté'* (*45,* p. 27). Why then does the narrator appear – for once – so unreservedly positive? For him these memories of past pleasures are as acute as the present one offered by the portrait and he is in no doubt that they belong to him: 'Je retrouvais mes nourritures à moi, mes joies à moi, faites pour moi seul, connues de moi seul' (p. 83). Sarraute herself intended the passage to be read as the narrator understands it. Her words (in conversation with the present writer) echo his: 'Il retrouve ses trésors à lui, donc il a la force de repartir de nouveau'. The narrator's claim may appear paradoxical, when the literary quality of these pages is so manifest. Indeed we may pursue the paradox further. If the narrator rejects the novelist figure of authority in the shape of Tolstoy, he has, we might argue, rival models or paradigms in mind. Some fifteen years before the narrator of *Portrait,* Gide's novelist in *Les Faux-monnayeurs,* Edouard, was similarly preoccupied with the conventionality of traditional realism and Gide himself was receiving Tolstoy-inspired advice from his long-time friend, correspondent and fellow-novelist, Martin du Gard. Other novelists, as well as Gide, made 'la rivalité du monde et la représentation que nous nous en faisons', the subject-matter of their fictions, just as the narrator may be said to do, or behind the narrator, Nathalie Sarraute.

Sarraute's fiction is highly personal, intuitive in its sources; it also owes a great deal to her early reading: 'I have been able to feel certain things and to try and separate and isolate them from a mass of other things, because my sensibility had been trained and my curiosity awakened by certain books' (*21,* p. 428). Dostoevsky apart, the books are above all those of the early modernists. When she discovered Proust in the 1920s: '[il] m'a vite convaincue qu'il n'était plus possible d'écrire qu'à partir de lui' (*17,* p. 2). When an article published in the *Times Literary Supplement* failed to register the ironic tone of certain apparently negative references to Joyce, Proust and Virginia Woolf in *L'Ere du soupçon,* she hastened to correct the misunderstanding in a letter to the editor: 'Il s'agit donc pour moi non d'attaquer les auteurs que j'ai cités, mais de suivre leur voie et de m'efforcer de faire après eux ne serait-ce qu'un pas de plus dans la recherche' (13 March 1959, p. 145). Such statements certainly suggest the adoption of models or paradigms. Where Gide is concerned, she has always been more ambivalent. But if she claims indifference to *Les Faux-monnayeurs,* she prizes very highly its predecessor of the 1890s, *Paludes,* with its anonymous, would-be writer-narrator who seems at the end to have returned to his point of departure. Moreover, if Gide the novelist was less important to Nathalie Sarraute than were other novelists, she is very ready to acknowledge a debt to Gide the moralist: 'Cela est un côté de Gide que j'aimais beaucoup; toute ma génération s'est nourrie des *Nourritures terrestres.* Elles ont joué un rôle moral très grand pour ma génération. C'était une libération' (*22,* p. 348). Does Sarraute, then, in *Portrait,* simply substitute one paradigm for another? Does the authority of the psychiatrist resurface in disguised form in a fervour modelled on that of Nathanaël? It is true perhaps that the umbilical cord which links the narrator and his creator to a particular fictional tradition is not entirely severed (as it will be in Sarraute's later fiction) and that here an explicit intertextual presence acknowledges this debt. However, we must beware of falling into the same error as the 'spécialiste'. He fails to understand the essence of the Gidean message, by taking literally what is meant metaphorically. He would, one may suppose, applaud Hubert's decision (in *Paludes*) to go to Biskra, while failing to realize that Hubert's mind is too closed to make the decision a significant one. Indeed it may be because the message has for him been assimilated, rendered anodyne – 'vous allez trouver probablement que c'est là un "personnage" qui date peut-être un peu' (p. 77) – that he offers it at all. But the narrator is truer to Gide than his mentor intends; he does recover a fervour but *à sa façon,* a freedom to develop in the way his own nature leads. It seems therefore entirely appropriate that, at this critical point in the narrator's endeavour, links should be established with certain novelists of the recent past, novelists who do indeed serve as models but only in the sense that they are perceived as agents of liberation. The parallels suggested with Marcel's discovery of his vocation and with Edouard's rejection of the mentality of the *côtoyeur* are very relevant and it is altogether proper that Proust and Gide should line up behind the unknown painter as further allies of the narrator in his struggle against the authoritarian figures of Tolstoy and the psychiatrist.

The visit to the Dutch art-gallery is not the only point in the novel at which the subject of paintings and art-galleries is raised. The central significance of this particular episode is underlined and clarified by an earlier passage and a later one, which link this particular painting, or painting in general, to the activities of the narrator. In the second section of the novel, when he rushes back to his friend with his new (as he thinks) perceptions of the daughter, he is reminded by the friend of an earlier exchange between them, when they had imagined a possible future incident:

> 'Nous avions imaginé que je flânerais un jour dans un musée ou bien dans une exposition quelconque et que je verrais tout à coup sur le mur, à côté du *Portrait de Mme X.* ou de la *Jeune Fille au Perroquet,* quelque chose que je reconnaîtrais tout de suite, à vingt pas, comme étant de toi, portant indiscutablement ta griffe, ta marque... Il rit... A côté de la *Jeune Fille à l'Eventail,* un portrait exquis, ton œuvre, comment l'appelais-tu donc?... ah! oui... c'était bien de toi... *l'Hypersensible aux...'* C'est vrai, comment avais-je pu oublier, cela me revient maintenant, *l'Hypersensible-nourrie-de-clichés...*   (p. 45)

Later on, the narrator accompanies the daughter to an exhibition of Manet's paintings. There he seeks to project the portrait of the Dutch gallery as a rival to the realist canvases they have before them and to explain his preference for its tentative, sketchy offering as against the large, solid, almost triumphantly 'real' figures which dominate the space of many of Manet's paintings: '"Je préfère, je crois, aux œuvres les plus achevées, celles où n'a pu être maîtrisé... où l'on sent affleurer encore le tâtonnement anxieux... le doute... le tourment...", je bafouille de plus en plus... "devant la matière immense... insaisissable... qui échappe quand on croit la tenir... le but jamais atteint... la faiblesse des moyens..."' (p. 192). He then cites the portrait as an example of the kind of work he means: '"il y a quelque chose dans ce portrait... une angoisse... comme un appel... je... je le préfère à n'im-

porte quoi... il y a quelque chose d'exaltant..."' (p. 192).
Through his evocation of the portrait, the narrator seeks to
make a similar appeal to the daughter and briefly – but only
briefly – thinks that his appeal has been heard. The hesitant,
stumbling words he uses re-enact the very tentativeness he
points to in the painting, thus suggesting once more the close
affinity between them and reinforcing the function of the
painting in the novel as *mise en abyme*.[5]

The tentative quality of the painting is partly what encourages and attracts the narrator, since it gives meaning to
further exploration on the part of others. This is of course
exactly what a work like *War and Peace* does not do,
according to the narrator. He may feel vaguely dissatisfied
with the character of Prince Bolkonski and his daughter, he
may even feel at moments that they betray signs of greater
complexity than Tolstoy has explicitly acknowledged, but in
the end he can do nothing but accept them. They are too
perfect, too complete in themselves to leave him any scope
for his own talents. In the state of mind engendered by the
painting, on the other hand, the narrator's own preoccupations can flourish; in this 'douce chaleur propice' (pp. 86-87),
a scene arises unbidden in his mind. Words uttered by the old
man seem to speak directly to him, 'Assez! Taisez-vous!
Assez!' (p. 85), despite the tenuousness of the actual link: the
original incident is now distant (and imprecise) in time and
place and was relayed to him by a third party in purely
fortuitous fashion: 'Une vieille amie commune, rencontrée
par hasard, m'avait raconté cela incidemment' (p. 86). In the
next section, the influence of the painting is still to be felt:
the narrator appears in the guise of an Indian fakir, conjuring
up the objects of his study as if by magic. We must now
examine in more detail the nature of the narrator's project
and the structure it provides for the novel.

[5] Lucien Dällenbach, in his study of the *mise en abyme, Le Récit
spéculaire,* Paris, Seuil, 1977, cites *Portrait* as example, though he does not
discuss it in detail. See also *40,* p. 67, and *43,* p. 55.

(4) THE NARRATOR'S PROJECT

At the beginning of the second section of the novel, the
narrator makes it clear to us, in tones of self-deprecating
irony, how the area of his endeavour can be identified: he is,
he says, one of those 'qui errent (...), craintifs, dans la
pénombre de ce qu'on nomme poétiquement "le paysage
intérieur"' (p. 26). We have already quoted the powerful
statement, at the end of the discussion of *War and Peace,*
regarding what he finds there: 'une matière étrange, anonyme
comme la lymphe, comme le sang, une matière fade et fluide
qui coule entre mes mains, qui se répand...' (p. 67). The
narrator – and through him the novel – is concerned to explore the structures of this 'matière', to familiarize himself,
and intermittently others, with it, and to examine the relationship between it and the surface level of ordinary human
converse. This latter level, though not in itself important
(indeed inauthentic compared with the authentic level of
tropisms), has a significant role to play in the novel. It is
perceived as an outer casing, a hard shell, which may inflict
hurt upon another or serve to defend oneself against attack,
but which by definition acts as container, vessel for a substance within. A number of images convey this notion,
sometimes stressing the softness within, more often the hard-
ness without: 'un petit nid douillet' (p. 41), 'ce cocon,
cette enveloppe imperméable' (p. 42), 'elle a retrouvé sa
coquille bien vite' (p. 38), 'leurs carapaces, leurs lourdes
armures' (p. 46), 'leurs carapaces rigides, leurs épaisses armures' (p. 166), 'Il a, lui aussi, sa carapace solide, son armure
où il est protégé, inexpugnable' (p. 160).[6] Related images
suggest heaviness, mass: 'un bloc solide et dur' (p. 65), 'une
masse compacte et lourde' (p. 124), or animals hidden in
rocks or shells: 'comme un bernard-l'ermite qu'on a tiré hors

---

[6] Such image patterns, with similarly ambivalent connotations, play an
equally important role in the fiction of Sartre, more particularly in *La
Nausée.* Sarraute's affinities with Sartre have been pursued by a number of
commentators; see, especially, *49.*

de sa coquille' (p. 38), 'comme des escargots qui se rétractent tout de suite dès qu'on avance un doigt pour les toucher' (p. 106), 'comme on fouille avec le bout d'une tige de fer pour dénicher un crabe dans un creux de rocher' (p. 37). This 'coquille', 'carapace' or 'armure' is a mask, a persona constructed and assumed to conceal the authentic life within. Father and daughter derive theirs from supporting groups, models to which they can conform: the 'fées protectrices' for the daughter, the 'vieux amis' for the father. A recognizable air, a style, a mode of speech goes with each, indeed constitutes each such persona. The father adopts a solidity of posture, 'bien planté sur ses pieds écartés, les mains enfoncées dans ses poches' (p. 165), as he echoes the platitudes supplied by his friends: 'elle n'a pas toujours été commode, la vie, mais enfin, on s'en est tiré, hein, mon vieux' (p. 164). The daughter, in her role of downtrodden, unattractive spinster, 'son dos aplati, ses jambes maigres' (p. 52), 'sa tête branlante, son visage plat' (p. 160), 'toute en deuil, avec ses gants de fil, ses bas de coton noir' (p. 155), adopts the words of 'les bonnes femmes aux visages placides': 'Elle est sa fille, n'est-ce pas? Et il aura beau faire, on ne peut pas aller contre ça ...' (p. 155). Such a persona is a 'déguisement' (p. 155). The text teaches us to be suspicious of all such surfaces, those presented by people, the father as 'philosophe naïf et désarmé devant la vie' (p. 104), or places, the 'petites rues assoupies' of the narrator's *quartier* with their 'maisons blafardes' (p. 124) and their 'façades flétries' (p. 158). It seeks to sensitize its readers to the activity below such surfaces. With time, we might attain the degree of control the narrator exercises, where the streets of his quarter are concerned: as with an optical puzzle, 'on repousse très légèrement l'une des deux images, on la déplace un peu, on la fait reculer et on ramène l'autre en avant. On peut parvenir, en s'exerçant un peu, à une certaine dextérité, à opérer très vite le déplacement d'une image à l'autre, à voir à volonté tantôt l'un, tantôt l'autre dessin' (p. 28).

What does the narrator discover beneath the exterior of miser and cranky spinster? Throughout the novel, he has moments of perception. It is, however, in the second last –

and longest – section of the novel that the narrator penetrates furthest into 'ce monde obscur et clos de toutes parts où ils se tiennent enfermés tous deux' (p. 180). He does so by means of an imaginary scene between the two protagonists, during which the daughter asks her father for a specific sum of money to meet medical fees. We are reminded, by the occasional intervention of the 'je', of the fact that the scene is the narrator's property, as it were, although he is not present. Father and daughter approach one another wearing the protective casing of their respective roles, like 'deux insectes géants, deux énormes bousiers' (p. 166); they argue and plead with one another but the words they exchange seem obscurely unreal to them, 'des mots de là-bas, de gens qui vivent quelque part très loin, comme sur une autre planète' (p. 168). Underneath the pleading and angry words is another level of awareness. This is registered by each as a summons by the other, obscure, unpleasant, provocative but irresistible: 'Un obscur et bizarre attrait. Quelque chose (...) qu'elle sent remuer en elle, un serpent lové qui se met à se dérouler doucement et dresse la tête' (p. 154); 'il lui semblait que des fils invisibles, collés à lui, le tiraient, ou qu'un enduit gluant étendu sur lui durcissait et adhérait à lui comme un masque' (p. 157). Images relating to unpleasant sensations or experiences, generally involving physical contact of some kind, re-create in the reader that sense of unease or even fear, which is the sign of tropistic activity: 'comme une compresse chaude, humide, qui fait affleurer à la peau le pus, mûrir l'abcès' (p. 158), 'comme une sangsue appliquée sur lui pour le vider' (p. 157), 'comme de faibles et mous tentacules qui s'accrochaient à lui timidement, le palpaient' (pp. 158-59). Such a summons may provoke a violent response but the violence will tend to rebound on its perpetrator; any pleasure derived from it will be of a masochistic kind: 'une sorte de jouissance douloureuse' (p. 159). Whether because of an original instinctive bond or because of proximity over a period of time, the psyches of father and daughter appear inextricably linked; hurt is registered as much by the aggressor as by the victim. To meet at this level is to abandon any sense of oneself as a clearly defined separate personality; the coming together is registered not as plenitude but as 'trou' or 'vide', the opening of an abyss, into which both protagonists, and narrator with them, threaten to fall. As the father asks the daughter to specify the exact sum of money: 'La trappe se soulève, ils ont soulevé la trappe, le sol s'ouvre sous leurs pieds, ils oscillent au bord du trou, ils vont tomber...' (p. 167).

Such mental activity, multifaceted, even contradictory, by definition constantly in movement, can be conveyed only by means of a scene in which the movement is recreated for us. Any attempt to label must betray: the narrator's earlier offering to his friend, 'l'Hypersensible-nourrie-de-clichés', is risible, transforming his living awareness of the daughter into a 'souris morte' (p. 49). If there is any one unifying principle underlying the characteristic features of Sarraute's fictional style, it is the attempt to avoid definition. Her abundant provision of semantic alternatives suggest that no one word or phrase conveys the correct meaning, her preference for clusters of images indicates her desire to create in the reader a sensation, while not allowing him any one label for it (for a discussion of Sarraute's use of metaphor, see *39*). From chapter organization to punctuation, all levels of the text offer an escape from excessive precision. The text is divided into sections, but these are neither numbered nor labelled; the use of *points de suspension* allows the sentence to resist the semantic completeness imposed by the full stop.

This tentative quality – which links the narrator's creation to the painting in the Dutch gallery – is reflected in the structure of the novel as a whole. 'Une fois de plus': the novel opens with what proves to be a characteristic phrase. The narrator is caught up in a repetitive, circular process, in which he tries, fails, cannot resist the impulse to try again, and, once again, fails. His difficulties are in part at least a product of the shifting, unpredictable, elusive quality of his material and the organization of the narrative seeks to reflect this fact. The narrative follows the narrator's gradual progress, through the ebb and flow of his self-confidence, towards the climactic achievement of the scene we have already examined. It is in the second section of the novel that the narrator confronts his material for the first time. In a combination of 'real' and imaginary scenes, the narrator encounters the daughter, imagines her going to join her father, rushes off to tell his friend of the experience. The attempt peters out in failure, but is interrupted by the sudden appearance of the daughter. When she leaves the café, the narrator follows, so that he can test his theories, not by narrating this time but by 'creating' a scene between them. Both encounters suggest the rebellion of living material against the death of fixed form or definition. It is when the narrator has successfully reduced his environment to 'cette place d'Utrillo' (p. 30), complete with benevolent old lady and whitebeam tree in bloom, that he suddenly catches sight of the daughter. Similarly, it is when the narrator and his friend have reduced his 'vision' to 'une souris morte', that she suddenly provokes them into renewed activity: 'De qui médisez-vous?' (p. 49). Ambivalence is suggested by the changing of roles on the part of the daughter in these two scenes: in one, taken by surprise, she is weak, in the other, she has the upper hand. Throughout, each character, including the narrator, is seen as a *carrefour* or a *nœud* in which a series of roads, or strands, meet up. Each is seen as being acted upon and reacting. Parallels and cross-references are established between the various figures: 'Pour elle aussi, sans doute' (p. 32), 'comme moi, tout à l'heure' (p. 34); 'Il a, comme elle, ces bonds furtifs' (p. 35), 'le vieux aussi, il est exactement comme elle, ils se ressemblent' (p. 46). Such a network of links suggest, on the one hand, the narrator's involvement in (responsibility for?) the activity he studies, and, on the other, the psychic interdependence of father and daughter.

When the narrator returns to his old preoccupations, in the state of renewed confidence produced by his encounter with the painting, it is the father with whom he enters into contact. Both Bolkonski and Grandet are more sharply defined, dominating characters than either Marie or Eugénie, and of the two figures in *Portrait,* it is the father who offers the greater challenge: 'tapi comme une grosse araignée qui guette' (p. 35). Anecdotes, memories, phrases, incidents, provide the narrator with material for a series of imaginative elaborations through which he seeks to explore what lies behind the solid façade of the father's 'avarice'. What psychic activity precedes his angry outbursts when confronted with luxury or lavishness, underlies his indulgent attitude towards the old or delapidated in the lives of others, explains the extent of his anguish when his own property shows signs of deterioration? That which appears on the surface as miserliness, is revealed as a kind of existential fear; the psyche feels infinitely vulnerable and seeks to protect itself against any manifestations of the ultimate crime, identified – tentatively – by the narrator as 'la Désinvolture'.

These scenes which focus on either daughter or father are in the nature of preliminary investigations such as a detective might pursue prior to his final reconstruction of the crime. The narrator's objective is his imaginary scene between father and daughter in which all he has learnt about them can be brought into play, and it is the gradual movement towards this scene which constitutes the central focus of the narrative. At the climax of the narrator's very first encounter with the daughter, we are given a first version of the scene, which stresses the schematic and inadequate nature of the narrator's present achievement: 'Elle se tient dans la porte... Et cela commence presque tout de suite entre eux... Leurs déroulements de serpents... Mais je sens que je n'y suis plus très bien, ils ont pris le dessus, ils me sèment en chemin, je lâche prise... Elle doit demander quelque chose, il refuse, elle insiste... Cela porte presque sûrement sur des questions d'argent...' (p. 35). The creation shades off into reminiscences of Green and Mauriac. The narrator outlines this same scene to his friend: 'je vois la scène entre eux, comme ils s'affrontent (...). La lutte aveugle et implacable de deux insectes géants, de deux énormes bousiers...' (p. 46). The friend responds with gossip; commonplace again threatens to triumph. The scene also figures as a central element in the narrator's attempt at self-explanation to the 'spécialiste': 'Je lui ai raconté tout, pêle-mêle, comme je pouvais, surtout la "scène" entre eux, ce moment où ils s'affrontent, qui me tire et où je tombe comme dans un trou noir' (p. 70). The chronology of the novel is that of the narrator's project, not of 'real' events. The dating of events, where there is any, is vague: 'C'était chez eux, à un déjeuner auquel j'avais été invité, je ne sais plus à quelle occasion, il y a déjà assez longtemps de cela' (p. 130). Various elements of the central scene are available to us before it is evoked in detail: the precise sum of money handed over at the end is already mentioned in an early version, 'quatre mille francs, les derniers quatre mille francs qu'il vient de lâcher bêtement' (p. 118).

In the detailed evocation of the scene between father and daughter, the narrator reaches a peak of achievement. We are reminded by the phrase 'leur grand bon fond' of the challenge represented by the true story of the woman of Poitiers: 'Quelle histoire inventée pourrait rivaliser avec celle de la séquestrée de Poitiers?' (*15*, p. 66). The narrator has, it would seem, successfully met the challenge: 'Je vois maintenant. Je sais' (p. 180). But even as he makes these apparently unequivocal statements, there are signs that his grip is faltering. The 'je' intervenes increasingly as if attempting to retain control of material which escapes it; the reference to 'la séquestrée de Poitiers' may itself be ambivalent and indicate a sliding back into the world of the *fait divers*. The apparent triumph of the first part of this section leads into the apparent defeat of its second part and the one must be read in conjunction with the other. The narrator has a further 'real' encounter with the daughter when he accompanies her to the exhibition of Manet's paintings. As they walk along together, the strong impression he has of her is comically whittled away: the words he finds to express it seem ridiculously inflated, 'une proue (...) une tête de gargouille' (p. 188), and he is finally left with what everyone else sees: 'quelque chose de discret, d'effacé, somme toute d'assez anodin, de plutôt insignifiant' (p. 189). He is then provoked by the paintings he has in front of him into a final attempt to communicate his own vision. He speaks to the daughter of his preference for the portrait in the Dutch gallery and tries to explain the reasons for his preference. It is as if he offers the painting, and with it his own perception, to the daughter. There follows an intensely dramatic moment, which perhaps, as much as the previous scene between father and daughter, constitutes the novel's climax. During this brief moment, the narrator has the impression of a response on the part of the daughter and believes that his vision has been re-created in her mind:

> Je me sens soulevé tout à coup dans un élan de reconnaissance, d'espoir... cette lueur timide et tendre, ce rayon caressant dans son regard, je le vois qui se pose, qui s'attarde avec complaisance sur une image en elle, celle que je vois en moi, celle qu'elle a aperçue, sans doute, reconnue en moi tout à l'heure, quand elle m'observait si attentivement; nous la regardons tous les deux, c'est celle d'un vestibule étroit ... on entend dans le silence menaçant des bruits furtifs... elles sont derrière les portes, elles guettent... il n'y a pas un instant à perdre... ouvre, mais ouvre vite, voyons, papa... elle tient le bouton de la porte, elle le tourne le plus doucement possible, elle chuchote, penchée sur le trou de la serrure... mais ouvre donc, voyons, c'est ridicule, on nous entend... S'il n'ouvre pas, quelque chose va se produire, quelque chose de définitif, de sûr, de dur, tout va se pétrifier d'un seul coup, prendre des contours rigides et lourds, elles vont surgir, triomphantes, implacables, dodelinant la tête: 'Voyez, je vous l'avais dit, un égoïste, un avare'... mais il ne le permettra pas, ce n'est pas vrai, elle le sait bien, ils le savent bien tous deux, il va ouvrir... elle le verra de nouveau, tel qu'elle le connaît, tel qu'elle l'a toujours connu, non pas cette poupée grossièrement fabriquée, cette camelote de bazar à l'usage du vulgaire, mais tel qu'il est en vérité, indéfinissable, sans contours, chaud et mou, malléable... il va lui ouvrir, il la laissera entrer, rien n'arrive jamais entre eux, rien ne peut jamais arriver 'pour de bon' entre eux, les jeux vont continuer, elle pourra de nouveau, serrée, blottie contre lui, sentir, battant à l'unisson, leur pulsation secrète, faible et douce comme la palpitation de viscères encore tièdes.   (pp. 192-93)

But the impression was false, contact has not been established. On the contrary, the narrator's approach is met with 'ce frisson de dégoût à peine perceptible qu'elle a maintenant tout à coup, ce mouvement léger de recul' (p. 194). Manet and Tolstoy have proved too strong: 'De bien plus forts que moi se casseraient les ongles...'. It is this defeat which accounts for the narrator's changed situation in the final section of the novel.

(5) 'MON FUTUR GENDRE: LOUIS DUMONTET'

In the second last text of *Tropismes* (one of the six which did not appear in the first edition of 1939 but which were composed between the years 1939 and 1941, very shortly, therefore, before she began working on *Portrait*), Sarraute presents a woman who sees the people round her (reminiscent of the 'bonnes femmes aux visages placides' of *Portrait*) as copies of characters from nineteenth-century fiction: 'des clichés, pensait-elle, qu'elle avait vus déjà tant de fois décrits partout, dans Balzac, Maupassant, dans Madame Bovary, des clichés, des copies, la copie d'une copie, pensait-elle'. She would like to reject them violently, 'les empoigner et les rejeter très loin', but they are too strong for her and gradually she weakens and gives in. The text ends with her joining in the game: 'Ah, nous voilà enfin tous réunis, bien sages, faisant ce qu'auraient approuvé nos parents, nous voilà donc enfin tous là, convenables, chantant en chœur comme de braves enfants qu'une grande personne invisible surveille pendant qu'ils font la ronde gentiment en se donnant une menotte triste et moite'.

The development of *Portrait* in general, and of the last section in particular, is very reminiscent of this text from *Tropismes*. Dumontet, though far from invisible, plays a similar role of 'grande personne'; he dominates and directs the other figures until they all, including the narrator, join in 'la ronde': 'L'œil attentif, nous suivons, comme des musiciens bien entraînés qui connaissent par cœur leur partition' (p. 207). Dumontet too is 'la copie d'une copie' and draws the others into the same artificial world. He has all the realist attributes of the *personnage de roman,* which the narrator lacks, and thus, in this novel's terms, no reality at all. He has a proper name, a profession, a social role (that of fiancé and future son-in-law), hobbies, plans for the future, a very masculine persona. His physical appearance is conveyed to us in considerable detail: 'Un Monsieur entre deux âges, assez corpulent. Ses cheveux châtains aux reflets roux, déjà rares sur les tempes, étaient lissés soigneusement en arrière. La peau de son visage aux traits massifs avait une teinte rosée tirant sur le mauve et paraissait un peu moite, comme macérée' (p. 198). He has large, white, fleshy hands with brown spots and short fingernails; he has a bunion at the base of his big toe. Thus equipped, he recalls the figure of Prince Bolkonski, with 'ses petites mains sèches de vieillard, aux veines saillantes' (p. 65), (or Grandet with his famous 'loupe veinée'). The parallel is further supported by the similarity of style and image used to describe him: 'Un roc. Un rocher qui a résisté à tous les assauts de l'océan. Inattaquable. Un bloc compact. Tout lisse et dur' (pp. 198-99). The short sentences and the firm punctuation echo the clear-cut impression created by the character. In his case, name, social role, outward appearance, appear not as mask concealing the life within but as a solid block. If there is life within, it is invisible. At one point, it seems to the narrator that he catches a fleeting irony in Dumontet's expression, but the moment soon passes and does not recur.

Dumontet's coincidence with his role and his resultant self-confidence are such that he dominates the others. The daughter has abandoned the 'bas de coton noir' and other signs of her spinster state. The old man presents him to the narrator and lets himself be persuaded of the merits of Dumontet's financial plans. Even the narrator is immediately caught up in the change of atmosphere; with a sense of being hypnotized, he greets the old man and his daughter: 'je me soulevais comme il se devait, traversais la salle d'un pas assuré, sans ralentir ni me presser, et m'approchais d'eux avec un large geste cordial de ma main tendue et un sourire bonhomme sur mon visage' (p. 200). Dumontet plays his role to perfection and the narrator's perceptions fade away under the onslaught of the surface discourse which fills the chapter. They are, as it were, crowded off the page. There is the odd hiccup of activity: 'Quelque chose a glissé, je l'ai senti, quelque chose a passé, à peine une faible lueur, un crépite-ment à peine perceptible...' (p. 202). But soon all trace has gone: 'Tous les trémoussements, tous les tapotements ont disparu comme par enchantement: en moi les petites bêtes effarouchées, les petites couleuvres rapides s'enfuient; je hoche la tête, amusé, je ris' (p. 206). The narrator finds himself discussing fishing and his uncle's apple-trees; he too has a physical past in the real world. Left alone, he and the father manage to continue the same kind of conversation, even without the supportive presence of Dumontet: '"Mais ces mariages de raison entre gens un peu mûrs..." Ma tête s'incline comme malgré moi, j'achève pour lui: "Ce sont souvent les meilleurs"' (p. 210). The words they utter have become neutral, 'Des paroles anodines, anonymes, enregistrées depuis longtemps' (p. 209).

By the end, the narrator's total reintegration into the 'normal' world is within sight. The lost sheep is about to be brought back into the fold; he will even be accepted by those principal purveyors of clichés who were so suspicious of him in the opening section of the novel. He will be able to settle down under 'l'œil bienveillant des concierges' (p. 42) in the décor of his *quartier,* and will listen to their judgments and join in himself: 'Ah! en voilà un qui n'oublie jamais de compter: un égoïste, Monsieur, un avare comme on en voit peu...' (p. 212). But the encounter with Dumontet is similar in its effects to the visit to the specialist. With the disappearance of tropisms, life itself seems to ebb away. Dumontet has a 'regard de Méduse' (p. 204), which petrifies. The daughter's face has 'cet aspect lisse et net, cet éclat un peu figé que donnent les fards' (p. 198); the father has 'un air tout ratatiné, comme vidé' (p. 208); narrator and father, left together after the couple's departure, resemble 'deux grosses poupées qu'on vient de remonter' (p. 209). In the future, when the narrator adds his voice to the choir of cliché-mongers, the whole world will take on 'cet air de sereine pureté que prennent toujours, dit-on, les visages des gens après leur mort' (p. 212), and the point of no return will be reached when he has taken one further and final step and no longer even perceives 'cet air un peu étrange, comme pétrifié, cet air un peu inanimé' (p. 212).

The last section shows the daughter, as is socially fitting, having found herself a substitute for her father in the figure of Dumontet. It is possible to pursue this substitution of Dumontet for the father at a different level of the novel's meaning. The father may be seen as 'turning into' the figure of Dumontet, as becoming himself 'la copie d'une copie'. This possible metamorphosis of the father from original to copy figures as theme earlier in the novel. When he lunches with his old friends, he takes on a certain solidity: 'il lui semble qu'il se remplit tout entier d'une matière consistante qui le rend compact et lourd, bien stable, "un Monsieur"'. For his friends, he has 'des contours simples, précis, un air rassurant de déjà vu' and for those at other tables, 'un seul coup d'œil suffit pour le cataloguer, tant il est, de la tête aux pieds, dans toute son allure, ses gestes – un type, un personnage, mais d'où, déjà, de quel roman? Ils ne savent pas très bien, mais d'un coup d'œil ils le reconnaissent: un bon modèle de série coupé sur un vieux patron' (p. 162). This is the first indication of future development where the old man is concerned. The end of the section brings this development much nearer. The narrator looks out of the gallery window and sees the daughter and beside her, 'lui'. He is recognizable by certain physical details, 'son long pardessus foncé, son dos voûté' (p. 195), characteristic details of dress and posture which have been identified with the father earlier (see, for example, pp. 97, 113). Yet there is something strange about him which the narrator cannot define: 'peut-être, dans les lignes de son dos, quelque chose d'un peu figé, de rassis, comme une sorte de platitude ou de banalité: une différence avec l'image que j'ai gardée de lui, subtile, comme celle qu'on parvient parfois si difficilement à déceler entre une copie habilement exécutée et son original' (pp. 195-96). The narrator's last glimpse of the father, before the two figures are lost to sight, is in terms which prefigure the appearance of Dumontet at the beginning of the next section. The opening words of the latter, 'C'est ce dos – ce bassin lourd', refer not in fact to the father, as one might at first suppose, but to Dumontet. The interchangeability of the two figures is further emphasized as the narrator examines the detail of Dumontet's appearance: 'Il me semblait qu'il avait avec le vieux, dans toute son allure, dans la forme de ses vêtements, comme un vague air de ressemblance' (p. 198). Both have, in particular, as the equivalent of Grandet's 'loupe veinée', the trademark of the

traditional character, a bunion on their big toe. It is as if to all
intents and purposes, the father had become Dumontet. Just
as, on the social level, Dumontet takes his place vis-à-vis the
daughter ('Je ne suis pas éternel. Il est grand temps que je me
fasse remplacer ...', p. 210), so, on the level of the novel's
psychological theme, Dumontet, the *personnage de roman*,
takes over from the father, who shows signs of age and will
soon die. What the narrator once saw as a mask imposed
upon the father from without, 'cette panoplie de carton aux
contours grossiers dont ils cherchent à l'affubler' (p. 168),
now becomes indistinguishable from the father's being. He
becomes his mask, 'la copie d'une copie'. Authority has, it
would seem, won out in the end. [7]

(6) THE STATUS OF THE NARRATOR

From the outset, the narrator appears as an outcast,
alienated from the normal world of human intercourse. Various references to psychiatrists situate him as mentally unstable, immature; towards the end, such judgments resurface
in the mouth of the daughter: 'Méfiez-vous, c'est très malsain' (p. 194) is her response to the narrator's attempts to
communicate his interests. He is perceived as a child in a
world of adults, powerless and inadequate, 'pareil à l'écolier à
qui l'institutrice place une règle en travers du dos, sous les
bras, pour l'obliger à se tenir droit' (p. 191). The narrator is
very ready to speak of his own efforts in pejorative terms: 'des
divagations de ce genre' (p. 43), 'mes vieux penchants morbi-
des' (p. 95); he is 'semblable au criminel qu'une impulsion
morbide pousse à revenir hanter les lieux du crime' (p. 81).
He is surprised at his friend's fidelity, surprised that he still
listens, 'comme s'il n'avait jamais remarqué ce que je suis
devenu depuis' (p. 44).

---

[7] But only temporarily: Sarraute's next novel, *Martereau*, reverses the
process by focusing on a 'character' with just the solidity of the old man
transformed into Dumontet, and traces his gradual disintegration.

We are given two 'descriptions' of the narrator; in both, he sees an image of himself reflected back at him, as it were, through the eyes of others. The first occurs in the second section of the novel, as he and the daughter leave the café and walk through the streets together: 'moi, trottinant à son côté, tourné vers son profil, avec sur mon visage ce sourire étrange, obséquieux, sinistre, niais, exaspérant' (p. 52). The other, more substantial and even more negative, is found in the second last section, as narrator and daughter once again walk abroad together, on their way to the Manet exhibition:

> J'évite de regarder, trottinant à côté d'elle, ce bonhomme 'sur le retour', à la mine négligée, court sur pattes, un peu chauve, légèrement bedonnant. Parfois je ne peux l'éviter. Il surgit d'une glace juste en face de moi, au croisement d'une rue. Jamais mes paupières fatiguées, mes yeux ternes, mes joues affaissées, ne m'étaient apparus aussi impitoyablement que maintenant, près de son image à elle, dans cette lumière crue. (p. 189)

On such occasions of critical self-appraisal, he feels that he is himself responsible for the shifting patterns he observes. The figures he studies seem to him an invention, a mere extension of himself: 'Si j'essaie, par un très grand effort, de l'évoquer de nouveau, cette image tourmentée, il me semble que, pareille à mon ombre portée, elle me rejoint, et, comme mon ombre quand le soleil monte dans le ciel, elle diminue rapidement, se ramasse à mes pieds en une petite tache informe, se résorbe en moi-même' (p. 127). From the first section of the book until the encounter with the portrait, feelings of guilt and self-condemnation are uppermost; they never wholly disappear, and dramatically regain the upper hand when the narrator encounters the daughter again in the second-last section of the book. Indeed it may well be his state of mind, rather than theirs, which brings about his final defeat: 'est-ce moi qui ai changé?' (p. 196).

In his self-doubt, his ambivalent feelings regarding 'la petite vision qu'on a couvée, plein de honte et d'orgueil' (p. 69), the narrator takes his place in an honourable company.

The psychiatrist, as spokesman for the normal world of ordinary people, makes the point: 'bien des types littéraires devenus immortels sont, de notre point de vue, aussi des névrosés' (p. 70). In *Portrait,* both Rilke (p. 52) and his creation, 'le triste Malte Laurids Brigge' (p. 30), are fellow-wanderers with the narrator round the alien streets of Paris. Another implicit parallel is with Thomas Mann's figure of the artist with a bad conscience, the *bourgeois manqué.*[8] The narrator of *Portrait* would readily concur in Tonio Kröger's ironic condemnation of his own kind: 'A properly constituted, healthy, decent man never writes, acts or composes'. Tonio would understand the narrator's contrasting of his own mentality with the practical, business-man's persona of the father: 'Il sait modeler à sa guise, dompter les choses autour de lui, les tenir à distance, au lieu d'aller se coller à ejlles, vivre d'elles en larve tremblante et molle, en parasite' (p. 88). The narrator's feelings are never other than ambivalent – or only briefly so, in the short-lived euphoria resulting from the encounter with the painting – but, in the sections following this encounter, the balance between shame and pride is arguably modified. The passage concerning the trip to the suburbs and the encounter in the station with the old man and the wife of his friend is particularly interesting from this point of view. Again the narrator has the impression that he has conjured his subjects up but he seems to feel as much pride as shame in having done so. He compares his performance to that of an Indian fakir: 'Et j'ai eu, cette fois encore, une impression de truquage ou de miracle, semblable à celle qu'on doit éprouver à voir les performances accomplies, dit-on, aux Indes, par certains fakirs, cette corde qu'ils lancent en l'air et que toute une foule émerveillée voit se tenir dressée dans l'air, droite et raide comme le tronc d'un palmier' (p. 97). There is irony in the alternatives offered, 'une impression de truquage ou de miracle'. Irony equally in the reference to 'une foule émerveillée' notably absent in the

---

[8] Sarraute read and was much impressed by both the *Notebooks* and *Tonio Kröger,* in the course of the 1920s.

narrator's case, but despite the irony, temporarily at least, the narrator identifies with the fakir's sense of success: 'Mon cœur battait très fort. C'était la même émotion qu'autrefois dès que je les voyais, mais mêlée, cette fois, d'un sentiment de satisfaction, de fierté: celui du fakir qui a réussi son tour' (p. 97). In the rest of the station scene, the narrator seems to play with the idea that the old man and his companion are beyond his reach, in a way that is comically reminiscent of Sartre's ironic comments, in the 'Présentation des *Temps modernes*' on the stance of the realist novelist, 'penché sur les milieux qu'il voulait décrire': 'Où était-il donc? En l'air?' The narrator reminds us that he is high above the platform and that, from where he stands, the smoke, the rain and the crowds of people prevent his seeing properly: the father and his companion are 'opaques dans la fumée' (p. 100). He is temporarily confident enough to make fun of the notion that the external appearance of these characters might add something to his knowledge of them; he knows that it is in fact his imaginative insight into their mental activity which counts, which makes of him a creator. The special relationship which he has with the old man and his daughter, 'ce lien secret, connu de nous seuls' (p. 137), is that of novelist and creation and the phrase, 'c'est moi qui les fais surgir' (p. 30), can be a source of pride as well as guilt.

The frequent references to childhood have similarly ambivalent connotations: the narrator may be seen as childish, incompetent in the world of adults, but he is also seen as childlike, author of an original vision which the adult world threatens to stifle (see *42,* for a full examination of this aspect of *Portrait*). The references to fairy-tales are particularly interesting. On the one hand, they suggest that the narrator's insights are not to be taken seriously, on the other they associate his endeavour with a narrative form in which the mysterious and magical are an accepted element and in no way considered to be out of place. The fairy-tale itself constitutes a form of *anti-roman,* a rival to the 'grandes œuvres composées' of which Sartre speaks in his preface.

By the end of the novel, of course, this self-confidence has evaporated once more and the narrator is only one step away

from total surrender and death. The opening section, however, indicated a new beginning, in the absence of any real
expectations of success, so we may perhaps suppose that the
opportunity remains for the narrator, like his creator before
him, to overcome present discouragement and try again.
Sarraute herself, in adopting the title of the painting for her
account of the narrator's endeavour, suggests a conviction on
her part that there has been a successful capturing in artistic
form of 'la trame invisible de tous les rapports humains', of
'the secret throbbings of life' (*21,* p. 429).

3

Vous les entendez?

(1) THE NARRATOR SUPPRESSED

IN her essay of 1950, 'L'Ere du soupçon', Sarraute argued that 'le ton impersonnel, si heureusement adapté aux besoins du vieux roman' (*15*, p. 68) was unsuited to the needs of modern fiction and that only first-person narrative supplied a satisfactory answer to the reader's suspicious question: 'Qui dit ça?' The narrator of *Portrait* serves the function not only of intermediary, directing the reader's gaze, but also of guarantor of the fiction in which he appears. He may also have served as scapegoat, a means whereby his author's responsibility for such unnatural, unhealthy preoccupations might be disavowed.[9] She herself has spoken of her choice of narrator figure as a 'concession au lecteur' (in a video film of 1973). Useful in the short term, he must in the long run stand between the reader and the tropisms he seeks to convey. It is noteworthy that, the closer the narrator approaches to the old man and his daughter, the more he himself tends to disappear from the scene. The logical outcome might seem to be that he should disappear from Sarraute's fictional world altogether, and by *Vous les entendez?*, this is what has happened. *Portrait* is a self-justificatory work in a way that *Vous les entendez?* no longer needs to be, and with the shift away from self-justification, intermediary and realist alibi disappear.

Already in 1956, Sarraute had begun to conceive of the possibility of an alternative answer to the question 'Qui dit

---

[9] Maurice Blanchot made this point in a review of *Portrait* published in 1957; see *32*; cf. also *44*, p. 183.

ça?', though only as a 'dream' not yet capable of realization. In the essay, 'Conversation et sous-conversation', she writes:

> Il est donc permis de rêver – sans se dissimuler tout ce qui sépare ce rêve de sa réalisation – d'une technique qui parviendrait à plonger le lecteur dans le flot de ces drames souterrains que Proust n'a eu le temps que de survoler et dont il n'a observé et reproduit que les grandes lignes immobiles: une technique qui donnerait au lecteur l'illusion de refaire lui-même ces actions avec une conscience plus lucide, avec plus d'ordre, de netteté et de force qu'il ne peut le faire dans la vie, sans qu'elles perdent cette part d'indétermination, cette opacité et ce mystère qu'ont toujours ses actions pour celui qui les vit.   (*15*, pp. 117-18)

The title of the essay, 'Conversation et sous-conversation', points to the essential element in this innovatory technique: dialogue. These subterranean dramas can be expressed not through action, 'cette énorme et lourde machinerie' (*15*, p. 101), but rather by the subtlety and variety of words: 'Elles [les paroles] ont pour elles leur souplesse, leur liberté, la richesse chatoyante de leurs nuances, leur transparence ou leur opacité' (*15*, p. 102). Moreover, since these dramas 'ne peuvent se passer de partenaire' (*15*, p. 99), they will inevitably express themselves in some form of dialogue. The form in which dialogue is traditionally set forth, which separates it off by paragraphing and all the paraphernalia of punctuation – inverted commas, dashes, colons, etc. – and the conventional 'he said', 'she replied', etc., does not, however, serve the purpose of the novelist interested in such inner dramas. For him the spoken dialogue is 'la continuation au dehors des mouvements souterrains' (*15*, p. 104), and there should be no brutal rupture between one level and the other: 'la transformation qu'ils subissent devrait être du même ordre que celle que subit un rayon lumineux quand, passant d'un milieu dans un autre, il est réfracté et s'infléchit' (*15*, pp. 104-05). The surface dialogue or 'conversation' will reveal the 'sous-conversation' or subterranean drama below; it will be 'tout vibrant et gonflé par ces mouvements qui le propulsent et le sous-tendent'; 'C'est insensiblement, par un changement de rythme ou de forme, qui épouserait en l'accentuant sa propre sensation, que le lecteur reconnaîtrait que l'action est passée du dedans au dehors' (*15*, p. 118).

In *Le Planétarium* (1959), Sarraute took an important step towards the realization of this new technique, by dispensing with a first-person narrator, and offering in its place a 'polyphonic narrative' (*43*, p. 84). The central figure, Alain Guimier, however, retains in some measure the conscious narratorial function of the narrators of the two previous novels even if he does so, as Valerie Minogue argues, only in order to discredit both narrator and act of narration. It is with *Les Fruits d'or* (1963) that even phantom narrators are dispensed with, and the 'sous-conversation' absorbs into itself the role of narration. In *Vous les entendez?*, the technique is further refined upon in one particular respect. Even in her early novels, Sarraute avoided the cumbersome attributions of speech which she criticizes in 1956; in *Vous les entendez?*, she stops using inverted commas to distinguish spoken from unspoken dialogue. In an interview of 1972, she said: 'I noticed in my last book – and realized it only a long time after I had begun the book – that I was no longer separating dialogue from "subconversation". That came about quite naturally. I even thought that maybe I ought to have put in quotation marks, all the same, so as to show that the conversation starts right there. Then I thought it didn't really matter' (*26*, p. 145). The close relationship in the text between 'conversation' and 'sous-conversation', dreamt of in the 1956 essay, has finally been achieved.

A study of the opening paragraphs of *Vous les entendez?* will allow us to examine more closely the distinctive characteristics of Sarraute's later narrative style, characteristics which derive directly from her suppression of the narrator and her foregrounding of dialogue.[10] The novel opens with a sentence which is apparently impersonal third-person narrative of a traditional kind (present tense apart), concerned with

---

[10] Considerations of space prevent me quoting the relevant pages here but what follows will, as ever, need to be read in close conjunction with the text.

an unidentified 'il': 'Soudain il s'interrompt, il lève la main, l'index dressé, il tend l'oreille...' It is followed by what we may assume to be spoken dialogue: 'Vous les entendez?' The rest of the paragraph repeats these two registers, first narrative, then speech. The dominant element is the speech: it draws attention to the laughter and offers a response to it. The narrative plays a supporting role, no more. The second paragraph opens with what is clearly a reply from a second speaker: 'Oui, c'est vrai...' The *tiret,* which stands before 'oui', suggests this and it is confirmed by the following sentence of narrative: 'Il sent comme ses lèvres à lui aussi s'étirent, un sourire bonhomme plisse ses joues, donne à sa bouche un aspect édenté...' Here there is, however, a new element: we are encouraged by the verb of feeling and by the disjunctive 'lui aussi' to adopt the perspective of this second speaker. He agrees with the first speaker, yet there is some suggestion of ambivalence; his facial muscles seem to act independently of his will and the result is not altogether pleasing: his mouth takes on 'un aspect édenté' and his cheeks crease into 'un sourire bonhomme' (a reader who comes to *Vous les entendez?* from *Portrait* will be irresistibly reminded of the hypnotic effect of Louis Dumontet on the narrator). We should not assume that the speaker actually looks like this, rather that such an appearance reflects his inner response to the words he takes over – with some sign of hesitation – from the other. The 'lui aussi' equally obliges us to consider the *first* paragraph in a new perspective: it is perhaps this 'lui' who is the principal observing eye of the text, and into whose line of vision the first 'il' falls. The dialogue of the second paragraph continues to indicate acceptance of the first speaker's response to the laughter, concluding with the statement, 'ils sont gais', with which the other began, but it also raises indirectly a query which gives some hint of future developments: 'Il ne faut pas grand-chose, n'est-ce pas? pour les faire rire...'

The next paragraph returns briefly to narrative, 'Tous deux la tête levée écoutent...', but its primary function would seem to be to indicate the source of the rest of the paragraph. What follows is what *they* hear, or rather their interpretation of what they hear. The opening words, 'Oui, des rires jeunes',

tie the response in with the dialogue, but the function of the
following list of adjectives and images is to convey a mental
response to the notion of youth. An element of narrative is
inserted into the 'sous-conversation', 'Aussitôt restés entre
eux ils nous ont oubliés' ('ils' and 'nous' have been together
and have now separated), but by means of an emotive response. There follows one of the imaginary scenes which are
such an important feature of *Vous les entendez?*, here intro-
duced, as is often the case, by a comparison: 'De ces rires
enfantins et charmants qui passent à travers les portes des
salons où les dames se sont retirées après le dîner...' A series
of evocative details follow: chintz loose-covers, sweet-peas in
old vases, log-fires, girls with dimples in white lace dresses. It
is these charming and innocent girls who are laughing: 'les
notes pures de leurs rires cristallins s'égrènent...' There follows the question, 'Vous les entendez?': the dialogue from the
'real' situation is imported into the 'imaginary' one. The
gentlemen sit over their brandy and listen; an atmosphere of
calm serenity and candour has been created. The last sentence, 'Ils se parlent à voix basse et lente, ils se taisent un
instant pour écouter...', forms a bridge between imaginary
scene and real one. We return to our point of departure and
to the last speaker, 'Oui, ils sont gais'. The repetition of this
phrase may encourage us to view the intervening material as
an exploration of the emotive content of that phrase and also
to see it as taking place within the second speaker's mind: this
is how he responds to the account of the laughter offered him
by the companion.

The dialogue now continues with a reiteration of the
query noted above: the speaker's irritation begins to be
perceptible: 'Dieu seul sait ce qui peut les faire rire... rien,
absolument rien, rien qu'ils puissent dire, si peu de chose
suffit, les choses les plus bêtes, un seul mot quelconque et les
voilà qui partent'. The next paragraph moves from what
could be direct speech, 'ils étaient fatigués pourtant', through
what could be either reported speech or gloss supplied by the
speaker (or both), 'la journée a été longue', to the re-creation
in the present tense of what must be a past scene (therefore in
the mind of the speaker?): 'Ils portent la main à leur tête', etc.

find
quote

The subsequent discussion as to accuracy of detail confirms the view that the scene is located in the speaker's mind: 'Un signe à peine perceptible... Non, aucun signe. Si, pourquoi pas?' The source of the next sentence, 'Le moment est venu, n'est-ce pas, où il n'est pas impoli de prendre congé?', is ambiguous: it could equally be seen as the content of the sign made by one member of the group, 'ils', to another, which is then 'quoted' by the speaker. Elsewhere such shifts – an integral part of the narrative – are in a sense more explicit in that they are marked by shifts in pronoun, from 'ils' to 'vous', etc., but this does not necessarily render them less ambiguous. The last sentence of the paragraph supplies us with useful narrative information, but information which can quite readily be taken as part of the speaker's thoughts: 'Le vieil ami venu en voisin pour bavarder un peu après le dîner les suit de son regard placide'. It is a way of suggesting, on the speaker's part, a sense that all is ordinary and normal: nothing has happened that is at all out of the way. In a different context, one might well be tempted to read the next segment of text as pure narrative, especially perhaps its central sentence: 'Sur la table basse, les bouteilles et les verres ont été écartés pour faire de la place à la lourde bête de pierre grumeleuse que l'ami a prise sur la cheminée, transportée avec précaution et posée là, entre eux'. But the 'maintenant' at the beginning of the paragraph and the reference to 'l'ami' half-way through, as well as the use of the perfect tense, remind us that here too the perspective on the material is maintained and that we should continue to read the text as discourse. The placidity of the friend's gaze, evoked in the last words of the previous paragraph, has infected, we may suppose, that of the father. Hence the apparent neutrality of this segment of text.

The opening paragraphs, then, are almost entirely devoted to a combination of 'conversation' and 'sous-conversation' of a three-cornered kind, the participants being the central 'lui', the friend, and the group of young people, present only through their laughter and the impact of that laughter on the listeners. Narrative is absorbed into 'speech', whether real or imaginary; we pick up the few necessary scraps of information incidentally, as it were. Characters are perceived as sources of speech, as present consciousness; indications as to gesture or appearance convey to us something of their (or others') affective responses, nothing else. They remain unidentified; 'l'ami' is, Sarraute admits, a concession to the reader and it is not until much later that the central consciousness is identified in so many words with that of a father and even then only by implication, 'il est bien naturel qu'un père se préoccupe de la santé de ses enfants...' (p. 51); we never discover exactly how many children there are.

In *Vous les entendez?* imaginary scenes have replaced the images of *Portrait* as the principal means of conveying non-verbal, psychic activity, and within these scenes equally, distinctions can be made between 'conversation' and 'sous-conversation', 'real' and 'imaginary' speech. In *Portrait,* of course, the narrator also produced for us imaginary scenes: sometimes what starts as an explicit comparison, 'nous faisions plutôt penser (...) aux spectateurs qui observent (...) les performances du gymnaste marchant sur la corde tendue, ou de l'acrobate s'apprêtant à faire le saut périlleux' (p. 132), threatens to become an imaginary scene, by virtue of its extension: 'Le jeune acrobate avait brillamment, avec une aisance parfaite, saisi entre les mains l'autre trapèze' (p. 133). Here, however, imaginary scenes are much more frequent and the distinctions between real and imaginary are blurred in a way which is very rarely the case in *Portrait*. Sometimes, as in the scene we have examined, there are clear signs of unreality: the introductory comparison, the change from 'ils' to 'elles' as perpetrators of the laughter, the slightly *invraisemblable,* caricatural nature of the décor. These and other indicators are used frequently in the novel but, frequently too, we are expected to distinguish simply on the basis of plausibility or otherwise. The shift from real to imaginary can be almost imperceptible; we only realize it has taken place when we are suddenly struck by the improbability of what we are reading. Sometimes the clue is just a change of tone, an increased aggressivity or excitement. The distinction is further blurred by the fact that no description, either of décor or of physical appearance, should be taken as 'real'; like the 'aspect édenté' of the second speaker's mouth, all convey an affective response, a momentary state of mind on the part of the perceiver, no more. Thus the elaborate imaginary scene has the same status as the physical detail which may at first sight appear to belong to a 'real' scene. Indeed a physical detail associated with a figure may derive in the first instance from an imaginary scene: this is the case for example with the friend's pipe. The distinctions between 'conversation' and 'sous-conversation', between real and imaginary, are blurred because 'sous-conversation' is made to dominate throughout. If the surface dialogue relates to subterranean dramas in terms of tip to iceberg, here the text seeks to reveal the true proportions. Indeed the dominance of 'sous-conversation', its tendency to absorb narrative, description, speech into itself and to use the form of dramatic dialogue suggests a reversal of roles: the imaginary is more real than the 'real'; 'sous-conversation' more outspoken and explicit than surface dialogue.

Equally characteristic of the novel as a whole are the shifts and ambiguities of perspective. A central perspective is established – that of the father – but we are left with the possibility of reading passages as originating in more than one source. Is the second speaker himself adopting the point of view of the first or is he only imagining what it must be? Is he supplying the young people with an attitude of mind derived from his own, or is he adopting theirs? Or are we as readers moving away from his and adopting theirs instead? We find ourselves asking such questions throughout the novel, sometimes solving them to our satisfaction, sometimes having to accept ambiguity. Indeed we must accept such ambiguity positively, as a deliberate and central feature of the novel's style.[11] This does not mean that we are wrong to say that the father feels, or the children feel, such and such a thing, but rather that we may *also* say that the father feels that the children feel. If we are not prepared to stop as we read and explore these possible alternatives, we shall lose much of the novel's richness. We

[11] Sarraute herself is quoted by one critic (*44*, p. 177) as saying that she does not know where one consciousness stops and another begins.

Vous les entendez?

have here the 'matière anonyme' of *Portrait*'s narrator: 'une même substance circule librement, n'obéissant qu'à sa propre exigence, entre des consciences sans frontières' – thus the *prière d'insérer* (written by Nathalie Sarraute) to *Vous les entendez?*

Vous les entendez? then is a novel in which 'sous-conversation' is paramount, to the virtual exclusion of every other register, and in which the source of any particular segment of 'sous-conversation' may be ambiguous. To express such material and to facilitate shifts from one perspective to another, Sarraute has found one particular narrative style suitable above all: that known as *style indirect libre* or free indirect speech, associated in the first instance with Flaubert but popular subsequently with those early twentieth-century novelists admired by Sarraute, such as Virginia Woolf and Joyce. It is a technique which, in its classic form, uses the tense and pronoun appropriate to a third-person narrator, thus allowing the author greater freedom of expression, but which also, by using certain of the normal indicators of speech such as exclamation or question marks or deictics (this, now, here, etc.), suggests that the thought or sentiment expressed 'belongs' to the character. Flaubert uses the technique in *Madame Bovary,* for example, to articulate sentiments which are undoubtedly Emma's and not his, but which she herself could not have expressed; it allows him at the same time the possibility of implicit ironical comment. Essentially then, the technique is one which allows for double ownership, as it were, of a particular segment of text: Roy Pascal calls his book on the subject *The Dual Voice.* [12] This duality is equally emphasized in the terms adopted by critics who have studied the phenomenon and its variants in Sarraute's fiction: 'discours prêté' according to Pingaud, 'discours pour le personnage' for Newman, 'counterfeit speech' for Britton. Examples of the technique are to be found in *Portrait.* Distinctions of tense do not obtain, because of Sarraute's use of the dramatic present, but punctuation, deictics and pronoun are indicators

[12] Manchester University Press, 1977.

in the following passage from the climactic scene: 'il faut
qu'on la conseille, qu'on la rassure, elle ne sait pas, est-ce
naturel, normal à son âge, ah! hffi? vraiment? qu'elle ait
encore tellement besoin de lui, parce que c'est dur, n'est-ce
pas, c'est dur pour une femme seule, et il est tout ce qui lui
reste au monde, maintenant depuis la mort de sa pauvre
maman...' (pp. 154-55). It is possible of course to suppose
that some such words are actually pronounced by the
daughter in scenes such as the narrator here evokes, and that
what we have is reported speech, but the emphasis on syntax
characteristic of direct speech ('c'est dur, n'est-ce pas, c'est
dur') and the concentration of clichés ('c'est dur pour une
femme seule', 'tout ce qui lui reste au monde', 'sa pauvre
maman') suggest that the daughter is adopting the speech of
others, which is of course the message which the narrator
wishes to convey. We have here then double (we might even
say treble) ownership of this segment of text. From being an
occasional technique in *Portrait,* as it was for Flaubert, it
becomes in *Vous les entendez?* an all-pervasive mode. As we
saw from the opening paragraphs, virtually all the text is
associated with speech, yet frequently imagery or improbabil-
ities suggest that it cannot be taken as actually spoken or even
as mentally articulated by the character to whom it appears
to belong. There is therefore uncertainty as to source. Equally, there is frequently uncertainty as to ownership. Shifts
from third person to first or second person draw the segments
of text which are syntactically identical to direct speech into
the ambiguous realm of *style indirect libre*: 'On se sent bien,
tout repliés, tout pelotonnés dans cette fragilité douce, lisse et
fripée du ballon de baudruche qui avec un soupir à peine
perceptible se dégonfle... Ah que voulez-vous, c'est ainsi, on
n'y peut rien...' (p. 106). This particular mode has a double
advantage for Sarraute. It allows her to exploit the imme-
diacy, the sense of authenticity, which the reader traditionally
associates with speech, while suggesting a level of response
other than that of the fully-conscious articulated utterance or
thought. It also allows her to suggest an interaction between
consciousnesses such that a given reaction must be deemed to
belong not to one or the other but to both. Such ambi-

guities do not explicitly inform every segment of text; indeed
the great majority, taken out of context, might, by virtue of
syntax and punctuation, seem quite unambiguous. But if the
mode is as pervasive as it is, it is because it works equally by
infection from a neighbouring sentence.

Thus we have, in *Vous les entendez?*, a technique which
provides the kind of direct access to the world of tropisms
which had been envisaged in the essay of 1956: 'une technique qui parviendrait à plonger le lecteur dans le flot de ces
drames souterrains (...) qui donnerait au lecteur l'illusion de
refaire lui-même ces actions avec une conscience plus lucide,
avec plus d'ordre, de netteté et de force qu'il ne peut le faire
dans la vie'. [13]

(2) 'MAIS QUOI TOUT? IL NE S'EST RIEN PASSÉ'

When, for the first time, the text explicitly posits a
relation between the laughter and the immediately preceding
scene, at the end of which the young people took their leave
(pp. 14-15), such a relation is immediately contradicted: 'Dès
ce moment tout était là, ramassé dans cet instant... Mais quoi
tout? Il ne s'est rien passé. Ils se sont levés, ils ont pris congé
poliment, ils étaient si fatigués... et maintenant, comme ça
arrive, restés entre eux ils se sont ranimés, ils se sont détendus
et ils s'amusent...' (p. 15). The whole novel plays on this
opposition of plenitude and emptiness, 'tout' and 'rien'.

'Il ne s'est rien passé': the plot of *Vous les entendez?* is
indeed minimal; two brief paragraphs of the *prière d'insérer*
exhaust it. In a country house, its owner and a friend sit
talking after dinner at a low table on which stands a stone
animal which – before the novel opened – the neighbour took

[13] This analysis of the narrative registers in *Vous les entendez?* owes much
to A. S. Newman's pioneering study, *Une Poésie des discours* (originally a
doctoral thesis presented at Besançon in 1971), which was the first to isolate
free indirect speech as 'principe d'écriture, lieu privilégié de l'écriture de
Nathalie Sarraute' (*44*, p. 99); also to the valuable work done in this area by
Celia Britton and Ann Jefferson.

from the mantlepiece and placed there, in order better to admire it. The sons and daughters of the house – again before the novel opened – have taken leave politely and gone upstairs to bed. Their laughter can now be heard through the closed door, stopping and starting again and again. The time-span of the novel is that of the laughter; with the dying away of the laughter, the novel ends. We know that the laughter is prolonged but nothing more precise than that; the friend's intention, according to the *prière d'insérer,* is to spend 'un moment après le dîner'. As the laughter continues, the two old men contemplate the statue, exchange a few words about it, other art objects they admire and about the laughter. The father, it seems, goes upstairs to remonstrate with the young people and they apparently come downstairs to reassure him. But the father's first visit (p. 16) is certainly imaginary (suppose he were to go upstairs, then the children would react in this way...) and the reappearances of the young people may be wishful thinking on the father's part. The distinction is not, as we saw earlier, in the novel's terms, a very significant one.

The novel begins with the father and friend listening to the children's laughter and asking what is making them laugh. Here too the subject-matter of the novel seems to evaporate before it begins. The answer to their question is nothing: 'rien, absolument rien'. This answer is one to which the novel returns at intervals as the laughter continues and the father responds to it: 'Un rien les fait rire' (p. 26, cf. also pp. 31, 33). The laughter is youthful, innocent, without ulterior motive: 'de vrais bons gros rires, dirigés sur rien' (p. 108). Perhaps if it ever seems otherwise, it is the father's fault; it is he who is responsible for muddying its clear waters: 'où a-t-il été chercher tout ça? Mais en lui-même évidemment. Chez qui d'autre?' (p. 26). For his friend, the young people are simply 'agaçants à la longue' (p. 104), and he accuses the father of wasting time and energy in speculating on the laughter: 'Quand il n'y a rien. Mais rien. Vous vous acharnez sur rien. Du vent. Du vide. Vous vous battez contre rien. (...) Ces rires sont ce que vous en faites' (pp. 139-40). There are a number of representatives of the outside world to whom the father appeals for arbitration in some of the more substantial imaginary scenes in the novel: a headmaster, a social worker, a counsellor, a magistrate, all people whose job it is to examine human beings, their psychology and their relationships, and to pronounce upon them. They tend to imply that the father is making a mountain out of a mole-hill. What does his case against the children amount to? They are guilty only of silence: 'Et quand j'ai dit: C'est beau (...) ils ont gardé le silence' (p. 101). The counsellor treats him with impatience: 'Qu'est-ce que c'est encore? Qu'est-ce qu'il y a? Toujours insatisfait? Toujours à vouloir la lune? A chercher la petite bête?' (p. 66). The book's ending seems to confirm such judgments. The last reference to the laughter (before it fades away and the door closes) emphasizes its innocence, 'Des rires insouciants. Des rires innocents. Des rires pour personne. Des rires dans le vide' (p. 185), and the whole novel concludes on the word 'rien': 'On dirait qu'une porte, là-haut, se referme... Et puis plus rien'.

However, such references to 'nothing' throughout the novel are more often than not ambivalent. 'Ces rires sont ce que vous en faites' may be a dismissive remark calling the father to order, or it may be read as a pointer to the need to scrutinize below the surface of things. The lead-up to the friend's remark suggests that the issue is a matter of choice: 'Il vous suffit de faire ça... sa grosse main balaie l'air... et il n'y aura plus rien: des rires de gosses. Ils s'amusent. Un point c'est tout. Des-gosses-qui-s'amusent. Rien d'autre. Ça ne *peut* être rien d'autre. Vous devez refuser que ce soit rien d'autre' (p. 139). This ambiguity is present from the outset: 'Dieu seul sait ce qui peut les faire rire... rien, absolument rien, rien qu'ils puissent dire, si peu de chose suffit (...) un seul mot' (p. 10), 'N'importe quoi leur suffit... Rien, moins que rien... des bêtises... des enfantillages...' (pp. 13-14), and, after the exchange which was our point of departure: 'il leur faut si peu de chose... un rien leur suffit... Quel rien?' (pp. 15-16). It is precisely this nothing – nothing in terms of external action, nothing in terms of the labels of the professional psychologist, nothing in terms of 'les braves gens' but 'un sentiment bien naturel de malaise' (p. 164) – which forms the entire substance of the novel. It is 'rien qu'ils puissent dire' (p. 10), 'vraiment ce qui s'appelle rien' (p. 32), but a nothing which, for the initiate, is full of meaning: 'Chacun d'eux sait bien, sans qu'aucun mot ait été prononcé, que des rires à propos de rien, mais vraiment ce qui s'appelle rien... (...) sont entre eux et lui les signaux qu'il ne peut manquer de capter, semblables à ces messages produits par des réactions chimiques subtiles et compliquées, élaborées au cours d'une longue évolution, qui assurent le fonctionnement d'un organisme vivant' (p. 32). No actions or words are necessary for the young people to impinge on the father's consciousness: 'il suffit d'un regard. Même pas un regard, un silence suffit... Vous n'avez pas perçu tout à l'heure? (...) Vous n'avez pas perçu dans ce silence comme un remous?' (p. 34). Nothing which is perceptible to anyone else: 'des ondes que nous seuls pouvons capter, sans que rien ne paraisse au-dehors, nous sont transmises directement...' (p. 115). It may be dismissed as nothing simply because there are no words for it; all the existing labels – 'innocents', 'moqueurs', 'sournois' – are 'ces mots grossiers à l'usage des autres, des étrangers...'; 'comment ces vieux mots sclérosés pourraient-ils retenir, enserrer ce qui sans cesse entre nous circule, si fluide, fluctuant' (p. 172). It may be suppressed by the 'grosse main' of the friend, or by a few firm and dismissive words from the surface world, and the father often begs for such intervention, but it is never suppressed for long: 'impossible de le contenir, cela explose-rait en gesticulations démentes, en cris indécents...' (p. 54). When this 'rien' is allowed expression, it reveals itself as intense, even violent activity. It is a 'souffle mortel' (p. 127), a 'couche de gaz délétère' (p. 117), which can make the father see his treasured statue in a negative light, reduce himself and his friend to stumbling, feeble old men with toothless grins, fit for an old people's home, or even kill them off. The first outline of the scene evokes its intense emotional content in rapid dramatic summary: 'la menace, le danger, le branle-bas, la fuite désordonnée, les appels, les supplications...'; the friend advancing across the room towards the statue is compared to 'un brise-glace puissant ouvrant, fendant, faisant craquer des blocs énormes...', what follows to the execution

of a sentence 'appliquée avec une précision rigoureuse par
des bourreaux insensibles au repentir, aux cris du condamné'
(pp. 14-15). The whole content and history of a relationship,
the closeness and the gulf between father and children, is
shown to be present in the brief scene which confronts
children and statue and sees them politely take their leave.
'Dès ce moment tout était là, ramassé dans cet instant...': it is
the novel's task to express this 'tout', to find words for 'ce qui
s'appelle rien'.

(3) THE PATHS OF TROPISMS

External action is reduced to a minimum in *Vous les
entendez?* Physical setting is of the simplest: the downstairs
room, the young people's room upstairs, and the staircase
linking the two. This simple 'realist' framework reflects
the novel's central preoccupations: each room stands for a
whole mental outlook, and the staircase for the movement
between the two. The room downstairs is associated with
the world of the father and his friend, with maturity, art,
timelessness, quiet; the room upstairs with the world of the
young people, with youth, life, activity, noise. These two very
different, apparently separate worlds are linked by the staircase, up and down which father and children pass: 'le père
monte voir ou s'imagine monter voir ce qui se passe chez les
enfants qui, de leur côté, viennent peut-être épier les adultes'
(*25*, p. 4). This physical movement, real or imaginary, symbol-
izes the psychological interaction between consciousnesses
with which the novel is centrally concerned: 'I wanted to
show a kind of interaction between consciousnesses which are
extremely close to one another to the extent that they almost
fuse and communicate by a kind of continuous osmosis' (*26*,
pp. 138-39). We shall now endeavour to chart this interaction
by examining the main thematic preoccupations of the novel,
the poles between and around which the psychological activity moves.

(a) /*Age versus youth* \

Already in the opening paragraphs, the opposition of age
and youth is offered as a preoccupation of the fiction. It is
presented by the friend as an explanation of the young
people's laughter, 'Que voulez-vous, c'est de leur âge...', and
speaker and listener are immediately situated as belonging to
a different generation: 'Nous aussi, on avait de ces fous
rires...' They are forgotten because they are old. The father,
as we saw, seems to adopt the role of *senex* with hesitation;
there are, from the outset, signs within him of a divided
consciousness. References to the father's age are frequent: his
'gros corps lourd', his 'bouche édentée' become leitmotifs
emphasizing the gulf between himself and his children. The
deliberate exaggeration of the toothless grin reference makes
it clear that no realistic physical description is involved,
rather an objective correlative of the way in which consciousness of age is a factor in the interaction between father and
children. Through the eyes of the visitors to the Louvre, he
sees himself as a 'petit vieux' (p. 183), when he attempts to
enter the children's world, as an ungainly elephant trying to
dance (p. 150). The young people are politely respectful, as is
appropriate, from youth to age, or alternatively gently indulgent of their elders' vagaries: 'il est très bon qu'ils conservent
leurs dadas...' (pp. 106-07). The young people are associated
with very different images, images of softness, freshness –
young animals, running water, green plants – and, on other
occasions, with the frivolity, carelessness, destructiveness of
youth.

ORDER e   A further thematic opposition, which is closely linked to
DISORDER that of age and youth, is that of order and disorder (or
harmony and disharmony), with the former linked in the first
instance to the world of the father and the latter to the world
of the children. This opposition is expressed through the
symbolic habitat of each group. The harmonious, calm security
of the drawing-room, with its muslin curtains, sweet-peas and
chintz covers is contrasted with the young people's room
upstairs, untidy, with objects piled high on every chair and
ash-trays overflowing with cigarette-ends, cluttered with

ephemera, records, magazines, strip-cartoon books. The precise details are not identical from passage to passage, but the images remain leitmotifs through the novel and one or other detail will suffice to evoke the whole mental picture. (Here we have an example of the kind of impressionistic short-hand which is a characteristic feature of the novel's style.) The irrepressible gales of laughter contrast with the quiet conversation below, the lively group (of uncertain number) who seize their magazines from one another, with the two individuals engaged in the contemplation of one unique and massive object.

The figure of the friend is closely identified with the 'idyllic décor' (*43*, p. 185) of the drawing-room. It is he whose words call it into being at the beginning of the novel and then, as we saw, the décor provides him with a physical object – his pipe – with which so many of his gestures are concerned and which contributes to the creation of a particular persona: 'l'autre, en train tranquillement de bourrer sa pipe' (p. 32), 'l'ami replace le tuyau de sa pipe entre ses dents' (p. 70), 'il tient encore sa pipe serrée entre ses dents...' (p. 129). The pipe is a reassuring object, connoting reliability and solid worth and a stable social world.[14] It may of course serve to conceal the inner uncertainty of an individual by occupying hands and mouth. The identification of character and décor is shown by the father's sense, when rescued by his friend's reassuring words, of being back again in these surroundings: 'vous n'avez pas quitté cette pièce si calme... les pois de senteur, les percales à fleurs...' (p. 53), 'lui aussi, tout comme l'autre, en sécurité parmi les percales glacées' (p. 117). The terms used to describe him also blend with the décor. He is 'placide', 'paisible', 'tranquille', he has 'des yeux candides', a certain solidity of presence, 'sa grosse main potelée', and he is 'inconscient', above all 'innocent': 'ce noble ami venu en toute innocence nous rendre visite' (p. 41), 'l'innocent installé paisiblement de l'autre côté' (p. 19), 'le doux innocent au

---

[14] In the light of these connotations, it is amusing to note that the cover illustration chosen for the Folio edition of *Portrait* is Picasso's cubist deconstruction of *L'Homme à la pipe*.

visage rose et lisse de prêtre' (pp. 124-25). The father and
friend belong to the same generation and they share the same
respect for inherited traditions, but the friend is securely
installed in his generation's values in a way that the father is

FRIEND not. He is a bachelor and views from outside, with 'une
expression de douce indulgence, de détachement...' (p. 53),
the challenge presented by the young people. He offers
reassuring statements in terms of the youth-age divide: it is
natural that they should have fits of uncontrollable laughter
about nothing at their age, natural that parents should not
understand their children. The young people's challenge may
be dismissed as 'Des révoltes d'adolescents comblés...' (p. 130).
His words, to the father whose grip on this secure world
is so much less strong, are 'étincelants de propreté' (p. 118);
'Comme tout est transparant là où vous êtes...' (p. 95), he says
wistfully and he pretends, as best he can, to be like his friend:
'il se tend pour respirer à l'air libre tout comme s'il était
pareil à l'autre, son compagnon innocent' (p. 117).

However, 'l'ami' is also 'l'invité', 'l'autre', 'l'intrus' or
even 'l'étranger'. Sometimes, he is an ally, appealed to for
help and refuge, forming a common front with the father as
'les deux amis' (p. 63); at other times, he stands apart and his
lack of understanding separates them: 'Je n'ai rien, mais rien
compris' (p. 86). He is an 'étranger venu de là-bas où règne
un autre ordre, d'autres lois...' (p. 42). From the children's
perspective, he is 'ce bon gros innocent sur la face duquel ce
sourire satisfait stupidement s'étale' (p. 112), and the father
rejects their suggestion that the friend is 'ton frère, ton sosie'
(p. 130). What he offers are clichés, 'ces vieux mots sclérosés'
(p. 172), that are reductive of the reality of father and
children. Like the other representatives of the outside world
– magistrate, social worker, psychologist – whose task is to
administer and codify the relationships between people, he
over-simplifies, he fails to understand.

Such oppositions, age and youth, order and disorder, are
relevant to an understanding of the relationship between
father and children but they do not provide a clear-cut or
reliable account of it. This is emphasized by the way in which
the value ascribed to each element varies. Roles in conse-

quence may be reversed. The ambivalence produced by shifts of perspective is hinted at early on in the novel. As Newman points out (*44*, p. 146), 'des enfantillages' (p. 14) could be either the father's evaluation of the children's preoccupations or the children's of the father's (or both). This same shift in perspective, and consequent revaluation of the opposition between age and youth, maturity and immaturity, recurs throughout the novel. The young people address the father in the tones a parent will adopt to remonstrate with a wayward child: 'Un peu de tenue, voyons (...) Ecoute donc un peu ce qu'il te dit (...) Il faut répondre quand on te parle' (p. 29). 'Un désespoir d'enfant' (p. 82) can be detected in the father's voice; 'Il baisse la tête comme un gamin qui a fait sa petite colère...' (p. 86); 'Il martèle faiblement leurs puissantes poitrines de ses petits poings serrés' (p. 156). Vis-à-vis the children, he is like 'l'enfant qui est venu près de sa mère recevoir un baiser' (p. 134); he has 'un regard d'enfant intimidé à qui on demande de réciter sa poésie devant le cercle de famille...' (p. 149). He and his friend wear the 'sourires béats de poupons gorgés' (p. 73); the stone statue is a toy rattle. Youth and age are grotesquely mingled as the father seeks to join in the children's activities: 'Il pousse de petits cris séniles d'excitation, de satisfaction, il ouvre toute grande sa bouche édentée, il rit aux anges...' (p. 73).

In a similar way, the opposition of order and disorder is an unstable one. For one thing, age is presented not only as robust, contented serenity, in keeping with the harmonious décor of sweet-peas and muslin curtains, but also as senility: grotesque, tyrannical, lacking in self-control. Moreover, the old people's interest in art is presented as a secret vice; age is accompanied by shameful desires. Father and friend let themselves go when alone together, 'entre vieux jouisseurs, entre vieux noceurs' (p. 114); the father indulges his proclivities in secret visits to the gallery: 'en plein jour, un jour ouvrable, n'est-ce pas honteux?' (p. 114); he is discovered by the children 'en flagrant délit' (p. 115). Age then can equally be a source of disorder. Thus conventional readings of the relationships of father and children in terms of youth and age are left far behind.

(b) *Art versus life*

At the centre of the father's world is a work of art, the stone statue of a mythical animal, to which the friend draws attention by lifting it from its usual place on the mantlepiece and putting it on a low table, in order better to admire it. It is the centre of the scene between father and children just before the novel opens and sits on the table between the two old men as the novel proceeds. It relates to the world of the father in terms of its age; it is an object of great antiquity, so much so that its origins are unclear, its precise nature unknown: 'elle ne ressemble à rien (...) c'est une bête mythique plu- tôt...' (p. 13). It is an art object, symbolic of the father's deep attachment to aesthetic values, the inherited treasures of the past, and of his desire to preserve these and pass them on to future generations, as his father and grandfather did before him. The father has done his utmost to perpetuate this family tradition. He has taken his children round museums, watched over them, protected them against bad influences, seized on the slightest sign of interest, coaxed them, bullied them, in general directed all his energies towards them. All, it would appear, to no avail: this is the drama of their departure, they turn their back on the statue after a polite show of interest and go away, to their own very different concerns. The laughter therefore may be seen as the children's response to the statue and the opposition between statue and laughter as symboliz- ing the central conflict of the novel. Even if the children are not laughing at the statue or at anything or anyone related to the statue, their laughter, even indifferent, still constitutes an indirect response to the statue and their elders' concern with it. The gulf between father's world and children's is empha- sized by the very different nature of the phenomena with which each is identified: the statue, 'la lourde bête de pierre grumeleuse' (p. 11), is all mass, solidity, immobility and weight; the laughter, in contrast, is lightness, spontaneity, impalpability, evanescence, and is associated with images of youthfulness, freshness and movement.

If art is at the centre of the old men's world, life seems to be identified with youth, a prerogative of the children.

Another opposition which makes this suggestion is that of the statue and the young people's dog. The two are linked by an identical gesture: 'il [the father] tapote, il caresse le dos de leur chien' (p. 28), while the friend strokes the statue as indication of his interest and appreciation. The father turns from the statue, 'cette vilaine vieille bête de pierre' (p. 35), 'cette pauvre chose' (p. 72), to the dog, 'la bonne grosse vie qu'on saisit à pleines mains' (p. 29), even at the risk of being bitten, in the hope of avoiding a confrontation with the children, and aligning himself with them. In the same spirit, the 'ventre soyeux', the 'douces pattes amollies' of the dog are contrasted with the 'matière grumeleuse' and the 'pattes disproportionnées' of the statue (pp. 29-30).

To the extent that the father's preoccupations and those of like-minded people are seen from the perspective of the children, they seem to point up such an opposition. All the activities relating to art, collecting, erudition, preserving in art galleries, are seen as barriers erected to prevent people having access to art, to protect it, as it were, against life. Is collecting a means of rescuing art objects from oblivion or is it to treat art as private property and to make of it the prerogative of the wealthy? Father and friend are referred to as 'les deux avares' and their attitudes sometimes suggest identification of cultural values with a certain class structure.[15] Are scholars less interested in their subject matter than in their own reputations? Do the supporters of art galleries seek to make art readily available to all or merely to protect it against the ravages of the uncultured mob? The young people's experience of art galleries is thoroughly negative:

> Ne les a-t-il pas assez traînés derrière lui, indifférent à la fatigue des longues marches à travers des galeries interminables, des enfilades de salles immenses, à l'épuisement des

[15] 'After I had finished writing the book, I ran across an article in *L'Express*, I believe, or in *L'Observateur* which stated that Mao Tse-Tung had said, "Art is the consolation of the gentleman", and I said to myself, "My two old men are like that", and that is how the young people see them' (*26*, p. 139).

longues stations debout, dans la morne présence, sous la
surveillance somnolente des gardiens, dans la promiscuité des
troupeaux de visiteurs amenés à chaque instant, rassemblés
tout près d'eux et soumis au tambourinement lancinant, à
l'infiltration pétrifiante des commentaires, des explications...
(p. 23)

The ultimate accolade offered to the statue by the friend,
'Elle mériterait de figurer dans un musée...' (p. 59), is thus
registered ironically by the young people as a commitment to
oblivion, 'parmi les sarcophages, les momies' (p. 60).[16] The
father himself has taught the children to see the ridiculous
side of an exclusive preoccupation with art: the woman who
spends all her time in London in the Japanese exhibition at
the Tate or the couple whose favourite memory of Leningrad
is of the Impressionists at the Hermitage. The unattractive
physical appearance of the latter, 'tous deux efflanqués,
voûtés, vêtus à peu près de la même façon' (p. 58), or of the
woman, 'la lourde fille aux ongles coupés court, entourés de
bourrelets' (p. 57), is contrasted with the impression made by
the children in one of those passages in which they are most
strikingly associated with life: 'Ils secouent leurs chevelures
qui ont gardé la fraîche odeur de mousse, de vase des
rivières ombreuses, ils dilatent leurs narines emplies de l'odeur
juteuse des prairies, des pelouses, ils ouvrent leurs lèvres
encore humides de thé, de porridge laiteux... et ils rient...'
(p. 58). The father's anxiety to educate them in his way of
thinking is seen as anti-life; it is tyrannical in spirit if not in
outward gesture (the bites cannot be seen), potentially hurtful
to the young people's independence of mind, hampering their
development or, worse still, stunting it for good, making them
into either polite nobodies or hostile, destructive louts. Lat-
terly, the father comes to feel that his whole anxious preoc-

[16] These critical attitudes are similar to those expressed in May 1968
when government cultural policy, with the museum as its symbol, was
accused of standing for the preservation of the old rather than the encourage-
ment of the new, for contemplation, rather than participation. But, as
Sarraute says, 'Le musée était déjà contesté avant Mai 68. Ce qui s'est
produit alors a catalysé mes sensations sans que je le veuille' (*25*, p. 4).

cupation with their motivation and attitudes has destroyed them altogether; he retains no sense of their real personality. To hear them laughing is then to emerge from a bad dream: 'vous entendez?... quelque chose enfin d'intact... c'est souple, ondulant, vigoureux, vivant...' (p. 169).

The ambivalent light in which the novel views the veneration for art which characterizes the father's generation, is further emphasized by the numerous comparisons drawn with religion. The stone statue is referred to on second mention as 'un objet religieux'. The analogy stresses the importance which art has for the father, ties his attitude in with a powerful Western European tradition, and also points up the abuses and distortions to which such an attitude can lead. It may, we are told, be a mythological beast, connected with some long-vanished religious cult. The parallel is ironically pursued as the father and his friend become for the children vestiges of a past civilization overcome by catastrophe: the statue is discovered by their side as 'un objet sacré qui servait probablement à quelque culte... Quel culte?... Comment retrouver ce qu'elle pouvait bien représenter pour eux...' (p. 129). The attitude of the statue's admirers is evoked in religious terms: 'pieusement (...) un religieux silence (...) pénétré de dévotion' (p. 17). Signs of respect are expressed in terms drawn from institutional religion: 'une brève génuflexion, un geste de la main plongeant dans le bénitier et esquissant rapidement un signe de croix...' (p. 40). The art gallery is a place of worship, and behaviour similar to that required in church is appropriate: 'son ton péremptoire mis en sourdine comme à l'église, comme au musée...' (p. 57). There are little upstairs rooms, 'intimes comme des petits oratoires, propices à la méditation, à la prière...' (pp. 180-81). The faithful make regular visits: 'les fidèles (...) ne manquent jamais les jours de fête d'aller accompagnés de leur famille faire leurs dévotions dans les galeries d'art, dans les musées...' (p. 127). The analogy is pursued in still more negative ways. The friend's bachelor status and his 'visage rose et lisse de prêtre' (pp. 124-25) implicitly draw on the negative, anti-life connotations of religion. Some of the comparisons suggest a degraded religiosity: the father in the art gallery is in a trance, 'comme plongé dans un sommeil hypnotique' (p. 24); he is given to all kinds of unhealthy, unnatural activities: 'les épreuves, les échecs, les désespoirs, les renoncements, les recommencements tremblants, les sueurs mortelles, les flagellations, les prosternations, les longues heures passées dans l'attente d'un signe, si faible soit-il, prouvant l'élection...' (p. 149). Other comparisons draw on the connections between religious institutions and the exercise of authority. The father and friend, inasmuch as they take on the role of priests, become tyrants: 'Qu'est-ce qu'ils se seraient imaginé, les deux grands prêtres, les deux tyrans?' (p. 61). When a divergent view is expressed and authority challenged, the response is violent: 'Si nous avions osé... Horreur. Péché mortel. Hérésie. Excommunication' (p. 78).

There are moments in the text which indicate that the father's communion with the statue represents an authentic aesthetic experience, that it is for him not a dead creature but a living reality. We shall look at these in more detail below. It is also possible, however, that the children's attitude derives from a new conception of art, a new understanding of the aesthetic experience and that the father's viewpoint is outdated and outworn. Perhaps respect for art and genuine creativity are not compatible. The children's off-hand frivolity, when, for example, they decorate the statue with a paper ruff, and their liking for ephemera, their refusal in other words to treat works of art as sacrosanct or artists as beings apart, may be seen as the expression of an attitude to art which is characteristic of the twentieth century. The reference to the Duchamp Mona Lisa (pp. 45-46) points to a whole tradition of argument: the Mona Lisa was of course an exemplary painting and Duchamp's gesture of adding a moustache became an exemplary challenge to the belief that great art of the past should be approached with reverence. By this allusion, the father seeks to dismiss the young people's interests as pale imitations of early modernism but they laugh at such notions of ownership in aesthetic matters. Their whole understanding of art is different from his and all the traditional ideas are for them outworn, irrelevant: the old myths of effort and suffering, the divisions into genre, the hierarchies of subject matter, even the belief in the value of permanence. The conflict between father and children is thus identified with the conflict in the twentieth century between an earlier but still persisting attitude which prizes art above life, as something which transcends time and death as superior form individually created, and a more recent attitude which seeks to reinstate life, to be faithful to its chaos and impermanence. The children, as they oppose the father, speak for such radical modernists as Jean Tinguely, creator of sculptures designed to destroy themselves, because 'to try to check life in mid-flight and recapture it in the form of a work of art, a sculpture or a painting, seems to me a mockery of the intensity of life.'[17]

A contemporary of Tinguely, who offers a particularly interesting parallel with Sarraute, is the Israeli artist Yaacov Agam. He too seeks to incorporate change and movement into his paintings/sculptures, and yet at the same time to affirm the permanent status of the art object and the ultimate authority of the artist. His works are, in his own word, 'polyphonic', expressing multiple aspects of a pictorial reality at one moment of time. In an essay entitled 'For a new written form of expression', he argues the need in literature, equally, for 'a writing in counterpoint', 'a multilinear language', which 'could express simultaneity and complexity, thus according with the mind and reflecting it more completely'.[18] Sarraute, one might argue, achieves, in linear narrative, effects such as those which Agam envisages. As with other thematic oppositions one can trace in *Vous les entendez?*, that between life and art never achieves a stasis. Just as the myriad pieces of the kaleidoscope seem to fall into place, so they are propelled into movement once more and re-form in another equally complex, equally evanescent pattern. It is this constant movement which characterizes the narrative of *Vous les entendez?*

[17] Quoted in Calvin Tompkins, *The Bride and the Bachelors,* London: Weidenfeld and Nicolson, 1965, p. 150.
[18] *Yaacov Agam,* texts by the artist, Neuchâtel: Editions du Griffon, 1962, p. 111. I am indebted to my colleague, Stephen Bann, for drawing to my attention the work of Agam.

(4) 'UNE SORTE DE PÈRE GORIOT MODERNE'

'Moi quand j'écris je m'amuse, c'est à la fois terrible et comique' (*27*, p. 13). The reader of *Vous les entendez?* is encouraged to participate in its author's ambivalent attitude and to find the dramas it presents both comic and tragic. It is as if the material were viewed sometimes through a telescope, sometimes through a microscope. From a distance, the frenzied antics of these consciousnesses appear derisory, out of proportion to the situation which provokes them. The perspective is not that of a cruel and mocking narrator but rather that of the characters themselves, temporarily adopting a viewpoint other than their own, usually that of the outside, normal world of 'les braves gens'. How must the father appear to the outsider when he rushes upstairs in an access of fury, as a result of some harmless laughter? As the elderly husband of farce, the wicked wolf in pursuit of the pink piglets, the sly fox who has got into the hen-house and is after the chickens. The imaginary scenes with headmaster, social worker, psychologist all draw on this comic discrepancy between the father's concerns and the comments offered by the outsider. The friend reveals himself to be comically unaware of the father's violent reactions: 'L'ami paraît réfléchir, rassembler ses souvenirs... – Oui, en effet, votre père a dit: "La quoi?" Il s'est montré surpris' (p. 93). When, on the other hand, our perspective returns to that of the experiencing mind and we see through a microscope, as it were, the material is deeply disturbing; the predicament of the protagonists, and of the father in particular, takes on tragic dimensions.

The novel presents the aesthetic experience of the father as genuine. When the circumstances are favourable and he is not inhibited by a critical atmosphere, he has moments of perfect communion with the statue: 'Dans le silence, dans le vide, maintenant, cela se déploie, tend les contours de ce dos, de ce ventre, de ce mufle, de cette oreille pareille à une roue de pierre. Ils vibrent doucement... des ondes s'épandent...' (p. 56). Art is a living reality for the father. But its life is

infinitely fragile; even words can betray and damage: 'de la
bête de pierre cela se dégage, cela s'épand (...) Même "cela",
il ne faut pas... c'est déjà trop... Rien. Aucun mot' (pp.
110-11). It is easily destroyed by a hostile atmosphere. In the
critical company of the young people, all the contents of the
art gallery lose their radiance: 'Tout autour de lui se ternit,
tout se rétracte, se referme, durcit...' (p. 40). As he turns back
to the statue and looks at it through their eyes, 'Rien ne vibre,
n'irradie, n'émane, ne coule, ne s'épand...' (p. 40); it is
transformed from a sacred object into 'Une pierre grumeleuse, d'un gris sale, grossièrement taillée' (p. 41). His wife
used to have exactly the same effect on him, as he explains to
the psychologist (marriage counsellor?): 'quand je suis devant
quelque chose d'où cela émane, s'épand en moi... quelque
chose pour quoi je donnerais... eh bien, il suffit qu'elle soit
là, près de moi, pour que je sente, sortant d'elle, comme un
contre-courant... plus rien ne passe, tout se tarit, s'éteint...'
(pp. 68-69). Symptomatic of his predicament is the difficulty
which the father experiences over the simple but central
phrase: 'c'est beau'. He would like to pronounce it with the
confidence of his friend, 'C'est bien beau, ça, vous ne trouvez
pas?' (p. 42), but when he is forced to repeat the words in the
presence of the children, his voice seems to him 'atone, toute
molle' (p. 43). He tries to make it acceptable by an off-hand
tone, 'Est-ce beau, hein, ça?' (p. 37), or even, 'C'est tout de
même rudement beau' (p. 40), or by applying it to dog rather
than statue, 'regardez-moi si c'est beau, ça' (p. 41). [19]

The father's aesthetic feelings are centrally important to
him. When they are threatened, he seeks to protect them and
himself by what means he can. But if this involves, as it must
do, concurring in a negative judgment on his children, the
'cancres' of the headmaster, or the 'natures médiocres' of the
friend, he finds this equally unbearable. His children are as
important to him as his art. He is thus torn between two
irreconcilable passions. His fondness for his children is ex-

[19] The radio play, which follows *Vous les entendez?* and is closely linked
to it in subject matter, takes the phrase as its title.

pressed through his delight in their affectionate gestures, his
awareness of their physical presence: 'Il sent contre ses joues
leurs fraîches joues rebondies, il hume l'odeur de lait et de
miel de leur peau, la jeune sève qui monte d'eux coule en
lui...' (p. 172). He is drawn irresistibly towards his children
and therefore towards the values they represent, 'vers ce
qui gazouille, sautille, se roule, se vautre, bondit, mordille,
gaspille, gâche, détruit, se rit...' (p. 35), and he has to ask his
friend to protect him against the temptation he feels to
destroy the statue himself and put the children in its place:
'on va mettre un disque de votre chanteur préféré, on va
ouvrir la radio, on va danser...' (p. 35). The moment when
they get up and go, leaving himself and the statue behind, is
for him one of acute anguish. Something in him is destroyed:
'Ils se lèvent... et en lui quelque chose se détache et tombe...'
(p. 43). He is like a speaker without an audience, an actor in
front of an empty house, someone who has lost his reason for
living. At this level of awareness, their polite leavetaking is
seen in a very different light: 'ils se sont écartés violemment,
ils sont montés, le traînant derrière eux, le faisant se cogner
durement, sa tête rebondissant contre les marches...' (p. 83).
When he registers the laughter as a sign of hostility or even
indifference, it becomes an instrument of torture: 'comme les
gouttes d'eau qu'on fait tomber sur le crâne des suppliciés...'
(p. 85), 'les notes dures, glacées, tambourinent comme des
grêlons...' (p. 26), 'et puis les rires ont recommencé... ces
longs rires comme de fines lanières qui cinglent et s'enrou-
lent...' (p. 146). His suffering can only be expressed in howls
of pain and fury. The nightmarish quality of the experience is
further conveyed by the father's changing sense of the children's eyes: 'leurs yeux candides' (p. 84) become 'des yeux
de verre' (p. 156); at times of reconciliation, 'les yeux d'enfant
s'ouvrent tout grands pour laisser couler d'eux et le recouvrir
des flots, des cascades de candeur...' (p. 51); when a feeling of
alienation is uppermost however: 'Leurs yeux vides aux
pupilles dilatées glissent sur lui sans le voir' (p. 82). Metaphors
relating to hospitalization and recovery from illness indicate
the extent of his relief when such ruptures are avoided, or
mended. Platitudes are sometimes turned to for temporary

relief: 'vivre et laisser vivre', 'des goûts et des couleurs', 'aux innocents les mains pleines'; they make the anguish of reality easier to bear but only by concealing it.

The suffering of the father achieves tragic dimensions because it arises from the apparently irreconcilable conflict of two passions, both of which are perceived in their turn as valid, genuine emotions. There is a further aspect to the situation which accentuates its tragic nature. It is because the father loves his children that he wishes to pass on to them – as a fond parent naturally desires to do – that which, in his own life, has been most precious to him. Why would the appreciation of great art be such a precious gift? Because it is, for him, the one means available to man of keeping death at bay:

> surtout de vous léguer ce talisman qui vous permettra parfois pendant quelques instants, sans dépendre de personne, seuls, de conjurer... mais pourquoi souriez-vous? – Mais on ne sourit pas... On t'écoute... – Oui, de conjurer... pardonnez-moi d'être grandiloquent... de tenir en respect la mort... (p. 155)

Hence his anguish when his children, in their confident and heedless youth, spurn the treasure he seeks to offer them. Hence his sense of intolerable suffering when, intermittently, he sees himself as responsible for their failure to appreciate his gift. What if it is his fault that his children have no defence against death? It is the existence of such fears which invests with irony and horror the vision of father and friend as petrified remains of a long-vanished civilization: 'Nous sommes les habitants de Pompéi ensevelis sous les cendres. Nous sommes des momies dans leurs sarcophages. Enterrées avec leurs objets familiers...' (p. 130).

There are brief moments of happiness when the father imagines a *rapprochement* to be possible, when the young people are reintegrated into the peaceful décor, which itself takes on thereby an increased charm and seduction: 'Sur les vastes fauteuils amollis les percales se plissent avec un délicieux abandon' (pp. 122-23). They are seen as creeping downstairs to look at the statue themselves: 'Délices inconnues. C'est quelque chose comme cela qui doit s'appeler le bonheur...' (p. 123). At other times, their worlds are experienced as shockingly different. The children seize their strip cartoons from one another: 'passe-moi... Non, attends, je l'ai pris le premier, non, laisse-moi juste voir (...) mais ne me l'arrache pas des mains comme ça...' (p. 61). The pictures in their books have no pretensions to timelessness: 'des lignes (...) toujours prêtes à être abandonnées, oubliées, satisfaites si elles arrivent à bien remplir leur rôle de simples signes, de jalons sur un chemin parcouru dans une galopade effrénée, dans un bruit de casse, d'explosions, vroum, boum, plouf, patapoum, tout bondit, vrombit, vole, s'écrase, brûle...' (pp. 61-62). The words are without distinction: 'des mots à tous, des mots de série, prêts à porter, des mots usés jusqu'à la corde, ceux des humbles, ceux des pauvres... plats et vulgaires...' (p. 62). Meanwhile the two old men, quiet in their demeanour, tender in their gestures, cling to the statue and what it represents, like seaweed to a rock: 'un obstacle placé sur le cours du temps, un centre immobile autour duquel le temps, retenu, tourne, forme des cercles...' (p. 63).

It is because such a gulf is unbearable to the father that his reactions are so violent. He registers indifference to his values as an evil, 'un mal caché (...) une tare héréditaire' (p. 65), which he must at all costs, if necessary by force, root out. Laughter, with its connotations of mockery and defiance, is, we might remember, traditionally associated with the devil. Hence the father's outbursts when he finds the young people absorbed in the kind of material from which he has sought to protect them: 'Il trépigne, il crie' (p. 82). It is in terms of the intensity of his feelings that we may understand his tyrannical impulses. He will starve them of other food in order to make them eat his: 'Il faudra bien qu'un jour, affamés, ils se nourrissent bon gré mal gré de ce qu'ils trouveront, la nourriture placée dans la cage du petit animal captif...' (p. 82). He will call in the police to force them into submission: 'Un bon coup de matraque par-ci par-là leur apprendra, à ces petits chenapans... Il n'y a rien de tel pour vous éclaircir les idées...' (p. 158). His violence is a measure of his suffering and his suffering a product of his love. He is, as Sarraute suggests, 'une sorte de père Goriot moderne' (*24*, p. 15).

The renewed comparison with a classic Balzacian character is interesting. On the one hand, the stress is, as before, on difference: here is a *modern* Père Goriot into whose mental activity we have more direct and detailed access ('what we know about reality has changed since Balzac's time...'). But the comparison has its point of similarity as well: in each case a father interests by virtue of the (excessive?) strength of his feelings. Goriot loves his daughters to the exclusion of all other emotions, to the point of blasphemy: 'J'aime mieux mes filles que Dieu n'aime le monde'. Even on his death-bed, when he has realized the degree of his self-deception, his passion finally reasserts itself and with it his illusions. Goriot is reduced to poverty and humiliation by his daughters, and suffers anguish, and eventually death, because he can no longer give them what they want. Though the father in *Vous les entendez?* does not suffer physically, his mental sufferings are often described in physical terms and the end of the novel brings with it a suggestion of death. His mental anguish derives from the fact that his children seem not to want what he has to offer, but it is no less acute than Goriot's: he too might be described as 'le Christ de la paternité'. Sarraute has succeeded in giving form to that intense experience of closeness and alienation which characterizes the relationship between parent and child. Her anonymous father-figure, through whose consciousness we explore 'l'immensité de la vie intérieure, l'infini que chacun de nous est pour lui-même' (*29*, p. 5), is as worthy a successor to Lear as was Balzac's 'ancien vermicellier'.

The latter part of the novel moves forward slowly to a bleak acceptance of the way things are. The father, in the novel's climactic moment, gives (or imagines himself giving) the statue to the children, an impulsive and symbolic gesture, born of his fondness for them and expressive of his whole endeavour as a father. The gesture is an embarrassment to the children but, not wanting to hurt him, they accept. Inevitably, they neglect it; in an attempt to make amends, they suggest it be given to the Louvre, where it will be well looked after. It is as if they rejected an inheritance which they found oppressive: 'Les autres, comme réveillés, se redressent, s'arrachent au bureau sinistre, aux murs couverts de dossiers poussiéreux, s'échappent, émergent dans la lumière, l'air du dehors...' (p. 179). The sending of the statue to the Louvre is compared to the consigning of an elderly parent to an old people's home: 'et surtout ne crois pas que c'est pour nous en débarrasser... le petit vieux que ses enfants veulent mettre dans une confortable maison de retraite ne doit surtout pas penser...' (p. 181). The analogy suggests not only the duplicity of the young people's motive but also the extent to which the father feels his own fate implicated in that of the statue. On the surface – and the novel moves towards the surface as it ends ('Et puis plus rien') – the whole affair becomes an innocuous and amusing memory: 'Tu te souviens quand l'un d'entre nous avait dit étourdiment que c'était une sculpture crétoise? Quel crime! Mon père avait envie de le tuer... (...) Ah, ce pauvre papa...' (p. 185). But the ending, with its shutting of the door like the lid of a coffin, also reminds one of the desolation of that earlier scene where the father had seen himself and his friend, through the eyes of the children, as inhabitants of Pompeii, representatives of a way of life destroyed for ever, buried under an irresistible flow of lava.

(5) CONCLUSION: STYLISTIC MATURITY

In 1956, Nathalie Sarraute envisages a novel which will plunge the reader 'dans le flot de ces drames souterrains'. *Vous les entendez?* is triumphantly successful in this respect. It describes its own subject matter in terms which reaffirm the earlier idea, 'tous ces mouvements de flux et de reflux, ces allers et retours, ces valses-hésitations' (p. 99), and brings that subject-matter vividly alive. Its success is due in part to the changed ratio of surface action to mental activity: 'Plus la craquelure de la surface est infime, inapparente, plus les drames qui se déploient sous cette surface et que la craquelure révèle sont amples' (*28*, p. 75). We are much closer to the material than was the case in *Portrait*; *Vous les entendez?* is more immediate and more dramatic. The narrator, with his explanations and his imagery of sensation has been aban-

doned; there is the occasional discreet, oblique reminder of
how we should, or should not, read the text, 'Mais quelle
naïveté, quelle sottise de leur prêter de tels propos... Rien de
pareil n'a été dit... rien de pareil n'est dit entre eux... Jamais...' (p. 31), but in general the reader is expected himself
to decipher the signs which indicate shifts from one perspective to another, from 'conversation' to 'sous-conversation',
from 'real' to 'imaginary'. These shifts are, as we have seen, at
times imperceptible, so rapid that a blurring recurs at the
frontier between the two. In the original scene involving
statue and children, for example, the father hides his face and
puts his arms round the children's knees: this detail, which
indicates his psychological posture vis-à-vis his children at
that particular point in time, is not distinguished from other
gestures which we more readily accept as 'real'. Similarly, the
dialogue which belongs to the tropistic level of exchange, 'un
peu de tenue, voyons', is not distinguished by typographical
or any other means from phrases actually spoken. The scene
with the social worker slips back into a rerun of the departure
scene with hardly a jolt: 'Dès qu'elle s'est retirée, ils essuient
leurs larmes, ils rajustent leur coiffure, leurs vêtements, ils se
penchent pour l'embrasser, ils tendent la main à l'invité...'
(p. 94).

This is one of the stylistic elements which give to her
prose its characteristic quality, 'cette sorte de tremblement
(...) qui est essentiel...' (*29*, p. 5). She has above all to avoid
any suggestion of stasis: 'Il s'agit pour moi de traduire des
mouvements toujours interrompus, en suspens, des sensations
qui se chevauchent, s'enchaînent à toute allure. Il faut faire
vite, c'est pressé...' (*29*, p. 5). Other elements, which work
towards the same end, are the very much more frequent use
of *points de suspension,* in preference to the rigorous finality
of the full stop, and the varying gaps in the print which
indicate mental shifts, while at the same time conveying the
interconnected flow, from start to finish, of the text. We have
already had occasion to refer to the use of impressionistic
detail ('Menottes. Paniers à salades. Passages à tabac', p. 80;
'Fossettes, roseurs, blondeurs, rondeurs', p. 10; or 'Estomacs
d'autruches. Gloutonnerie. Avidité', p. 75) which, as well as

stressing the unreal, symbolic function of such detail, speeds up the process of establishing the particular psychological moment in question.

In such lists as we have just quoted, a sensitive awareness of language is clearly operative; assonance and alliteration motivate the choice of words and the links thus established between one word or phrase and the next become a means of suggesting, with great lightness of touch, the shifting, complex nature of the psychological material which is being explored. As we saw at the beginning of our discussion of *Vous les entendez?*, there is in Sarraute's later novels a significant shift towards *speech* as a means of expressing tropisms. Sarraute's radio plays have tended to be regarded as existing in the shadow of her fiction, in part because she herself was initially resistant to the idea that she could write for a different medium. It is interesting to note, however, that her first play dates from the same period as *Les Fruits d'or,* the novel in which arguably she finds her mature voice. While she has been happy to approve the transfer of her plays from radio to theatre and to interest herself in their staging, she herself wonders whether they gain anything thereby or whether they may even lose something of their impact. What she said in relation to the staging of *Le Silence* and *Le Mensonge* is true of all her plays and increasingly, one might say, of her fiction: 'I don't visualize any characters (...) I don't see any exterior action. I just hear voices and rhythms' (*26,* p. 146). Both plays and novels seek to give expression to what it is that she hears. She disputes Sartre's view (as expressed in the preface to *Portrait*) that she is interested in 'la banalité et l'inauthenticité de l'échange oral. (...) Ce qui m'intéresse, ce n'est pas l'inconsistance apparente des bavardages, c'est précisément la consistance inconnue mais sensible dont ils sont lourds (...). Les clichés, les lieux communs, il n'y a que ça dans la vie courante, pourquoi taper dessus? Il n'y a même pas à s'en méfier: s'il fait beau, il fait beau. Ce qui est intéressant, c'est de savoir pourquoi je vais dire ça à mon voisin, sur quel ton, etc.' (*29,* p. 5). It is this awareness of hidden layers of meaning, this sensitivity of ear, which she tries to re-create in her readers, and which make of her a poetic novelist of extraordinary subtlety and richness. 'Alors que se passe-t-il?' asks the *prière d'insérer* to *Vous les entendez?* and answers, 'Rien qui puisse être transmis autrement que par le texte même'. We have tried here to emulate the reader of good will: 'celui qui voudra bien l'aider à vivre'.

Canterbury, 1985

Select Bibliography

F O R a full listing of work by and on Nathalie Sarraute, see Sheila M. Bell, *Nathalie Sarraute: a bibliography* (Research Bibliographies and Checklists), London: Grant and Cutler, 1982.

I. WORKS BY NATHALIE SARRAUTE

(a) *Fiction*

1. *Tropismes*, Paris: Denoël, 1939.
2. *Portrait d'un inconnu*, Paris: Robert Marin, 1948.
3. *Martereau*, Paris: Gallimard, 1953.
4. *Le Planétarium*, Paris: Gallimard, 1959.
5. *Les Fruits d'or*, Paris: Gallimard, 1963.
6. *Entre la vie et la mort*, Paris: Gallimard, 1968.
7. *Vous les entendez?*, Paris: Gallimard, 1972.
8. *'disent les imbéciles'*, Paris: Gallimard, 1976.
9. *L'Usage de la parole*, Paris: Gallimard, 1980.

(b) *Plays*

10. *Le Silence*, suivi de *Le Mensonge*, Paris: Gallimard, 1967.
11. *Isma ou ce qui s'appelle rien*, suivi de *Le Silence* et *Le Mensonge* (Le Manteau d'Arlequin), Paris: Gallimard, 1970.
12. *Théâtre* (contains the above, *C'est beau* and *Elle est là*), Paris: Gallimard, 1978.
13. *Pour un oui ou pour un non*, Paris: Gallimard, 1982.

(c) *Autobiography*

14. *Enfance*, Paris: Gallimard, 1983.

(d) *Essays, interviews, etc., referred to in this volume*

15. *L'Ere du soupçon* (Les Essais), Paris: Gallimard, 1956.
16. *L'Ere du soupçon* (Idées), Paris: Gallimard, 1964 (with a preface by Sarraute).
17. Demeron, Pierre, 'Nathalie Sarraute ou littérature sans cabotinage', *Arts* (3.6.59), 2.

18. Bourdet, Denise, 'Nathalie Sarraute', pp. 58-63, in *Visages d'aujourd'hui*, Paris: Plon, 1960.
19. 'Rebels in a World of Platitudes', *Times Literary Supplement* (10.6.60), 371.
20. 'Tolstoï', *Les Lettres françaises* (22.9.60), 1, 7.
21. 'New Movements in French Literature: Nathalie Sarraute explains tropisms', *The Listener* (9.3.61), 428-29.
22. 'Interview de Nathalie Sarraute', pp. 343-54, in Margaret Boulle, 'La Remise en question du personnage, *Les Faux-monnayeurs* et le nouveau roman', thèse de doctorat de l'Université de Paris (Sorbonne), 1969.
23. 'Ce que je cherche à faire', pp. 25-40, in *Nouveau roman: hier, aujourd'hui*, II: *Pratiques*, ed. Jean Ricardou (10/18), Paris: Union Générale d'Editions, 1972.
24. 'Nathalie Sarraute a réponse à tous'. Présenté par Bernard Pivot, *Le Figaro* (4.2.72), 13, 15.
25. Le Clec'h, Guy, 'Entretien avec Nathalie Sarraute. Drames microscopiques', *Les Nouvelles littéraires* (28.2.72), 4-5.
26. Brée, Germaine, 'Nathalie Sarraute', *Contemporary Literature*, XIV, 2 (Spring 1973), 137-46.
27. 'Nathalie Sarraute'. Entretien par Simone Benmussa, *Combat* (14.3.74), 13.
28. 'Le gant retourné', *Cahiers Renaud Barrault*, 89 (1975), 70-79.
29. 'Nathalie Sarraute: "Sartre s'est trompé à mon sujet"'. Propos recueillis par Jean-Louis Ezine, *Les Nouvelles littéraires* (30.9.76), 5.

II. Critical works

30. Besser, Gretchen Rous, *Nathalie Sarraute* (Twayne's World Authors Series), New York: Twayne, 1979.
31. Bernal, Olga, 'Des fiches et des fluides dans le roman de Nathalie Sarraute', *MLN*, LXXXVIII, 4 (May 1973), 775-88.
32. Blanchot, Maurice, 'D'un art sans avenir', *NNRF*, IX, 51 (March 1957), 488-98.
33. Britton, Celia, 'The Function of the Commonplace in the Novels of Nathalie Sarraute', *Language and Style*, XII, 2 (Spring 1979), 79-90.
34. ———, 'The Self and Language in the Novels of Nathalie Sarraute', *Modern Language Review*, LXXVII, 3 (July 1982), 577-84.
35. ———, 'Reported Speech and Sous-conversation: Forms of Intersubjectivity in Nathalie Sarraute's Novels', *Romance Studies*, 2 (Summer 1983), 69-79.
36. Calin, Françoise, *La Vie retrouvée. Etude de l'œuvre romanesque de Nathalie Sarraute* (Situation), Paris: Lettres modernes Minard, 1976.
37. Cranaki, Mimica and Yvon Belaval, *Nathalie Sarraute* (Bibliothèque idéale), Paris: Gallimard, 1965.

38. Jefferson, Ann, 'What's in a Name? From Surname to Pronoun in the Novels of Nathalie Sarraute', *PTL: a journal for descriptive poetics and theory of literature,* II, 2 (April 1977), 203-20.

39. ———, 'Imagery versus Description: the Problematics of Representation in the Novels of Nathalie Sarraute', *Modern Language Review,* LXXIII, 3 (July 1978), 513-24.

40. ———, *The Nouveau Roman and the Poetics of Fiction,* Cambridge: Cambridge University Press, 1980.

41. Le Huenen, Roland, 'Objets et société dans *Vous les entendez?* de Nathalie Sarraute', pp. 249-61, in *La Lecture socio-critique du texte romanesque,* ed. Graham Falconer and Henri Mitterand, Toronto: Samuel Stevens, Hakkert and Company, 1975.

42. Minogue, Valerie, 'The Imagery of Childhood in Nathalie Sarraute's *Portrait d'un inconnu',* French Studies, XXVII, 2 (April 1973), 177-86.

43. ———, *Nathalie Sarraute and the War of the Words,* Edinburgh: Edinburgh University Press, 1981.

44. Newman, A. S., *Une Poésie des discours. Essai sur les romans de Nathalie Sarraute* (Histoire des idées et critique littéraire), Geneva: Droz, 1976.

45. Pingaud, Bernard, 'Le personnage dans l'œuvre de Nathalie Sarraute', *Preuves,* XIII, 154 (Dec. 1963), 19-34.

46. Saint-Amour, David, 'Cyclical Structure in the Novels of Nathalie Sarraute', *Michigan Academician,* VIII (1975), 29-37.

47. Schwamborn-Kuske, Ingrid, *Nathalie Sarraute: 'Portrait d'un inconnu'* (Literatur im Dialog, 6), Munich: Fink, 1975.

48. Tison Braun, Micheline, *Nathalie Sarraute ou la recherche de l'authenticité,* Paris: Gallimard, 1971.

49. Wunderli-Müller, Christine B., *Le Thème du masque et les banalités dans l'œuvre de Nathalie Sarraute,* Zurich: Juris, 1970.

CRITICAL GUIDES TO FRENCH TEXTS

edited by
Roger Little, Wolfgang van Emden, David Williams